Skills for **Employability**

Step UP

C1

Coursebook and **eBook**

Iwonna Dubicka
Margaret O'Keeffe
Marjorie Rosenberg

Step Up C1

Pearson Education, 221 River Street, Hoboken, NJ 07030 USA

Cover Illustration: Roy Hermelin

Text composition: Straive

Library of Congress Cataloging-in-Publication Data: A catalog record for the print edition is available from the Library of Congress.

Printed in the United States of America

ISBN-13: 978-0-13-747371-7

1 2023

Acknowledgments

We would like to thank the following people for their help with this project.

Güzide Göksen Birol, Istanbul Okan University; **Eduardo Pinell Campuzano,** CIU Director, Universidad Privada Franz Tamayo; **Meg Cassamally,** University of Siena; **Adrian Crawley,** Evority Learning Centre; University of Siena; **Yabancı Diller,** School of Foreign Languages; **Louise Dixon,** Director of Studies at Hallo! Servizi Linguistici; **Aybala Eren,** Gazi University; **Alex Fayle,** Well & Will Language Academy; **Elizabeth Cruz Flores,** Tecnológico de Monterrey; **Jacques Friggieri,** Redrob; **María Amparo Garcia,** ICPNA Cusco; **Christina Gebbia,** Director of Let's Talk English Center in Valencia; **Maria de la Paz Giglio,** New Concept School of English; **Zeynep Güler,** İstanbul Okan University; **Ilaria Incorvaia,** ITIS 'Antonio Meucci', Florence; **Nancy Johnstone,** School of Engineering, UBA, Buenos Aires, Argentina; **Sevil Altıkulaçoğlu Kayaer,** Gazi University; **Yeliz Korkmaz,** Yıldız Technical University, Turkey; **Héctor Raúl Sánchez Lozano,** Proulex Universidad de Guadalajara; **Mariana Juana Aviles Martillo,** coordinator of CEFI, Center for Continuing Educatiòn and Interamerican Labor; **Anne Marie Mc Gowan,** University of Rome' Tor Vergata' Italy; **Cristian Meléndez,** Universidad Católica de El Salvador; **Jose Manuel Mendivil S.,** Centro Boliviano Americano - Fundación Cultural y Educativa La Paz; **Paul Cruz Montenegro,** English Coordinator of CRC - Peru Cruceros; **M.Àngels Nogué,** Centre D'Idiomes Olot; **Irem Ozcan,** Gazi University, College of Foreign Languages; **Claudia Posarelli,** ITIS Meucci Firenze; **Steven Pragnell,** Astex Servicios Lingüísticos, Madrid; **María de Lourdes Camarillo Rodríguez,** Escuela Bancaria y Comercial; **Raquel Sánchez,** Faculty of Education in Albacete (UCLM); **Chayapak Tangapiwut,** Burapha University Language Institute; **Onur Uludag,** Yildiz Technical University; **Taku Umeda,** Tokyo Business and Language College; **Laura Vacca,** Inglese su Misura; **Marijke van Leuven,** Oxford School of English, Verona, Italy.

Photo Credits Page 2: Rawpixel.com/Shutterstock; 5: New Africa/Shutterstock; 7 (Oscar): Jack Frog/Shutterstock; 7 (Kent): Diana Grytsku/Shutterstock; 7 (Shivaya): Ground Picture/Shutterstock; 7 (Rosa): BearFotos/Shutterstock; 8: Viktoria Kurpas/Shutterstock; 9: Gorodenkoff/Shutterstock; 11: New Africa/Shutterstock; 12: MD. Delwar hossain/Shutterstock; 13: Studio Romantic; 15: MediaGroup_BestForYou/Shutterstock; 16 (innovation): Garagestock/Shutterstock; 16 (engagement): Garagestock/Shutterstock; 16 (goals): Garagestock/Shutterstock; 16 (employees): Garagestock/Shutterstock; 17: Roman Samborskyi/Shutterstock; 18 (Astrid): Chadchai Krisadapong/Shutterstock; 19 (Sterling): Prostock-studio/Shutterstock; 19 (Camila): Ground Picture/Shutterstock; 20: Kachka/Shutterstock; 21: Mangpor2004/Shutterstock; 23 (empathize): Pgvector/Shutterstock; 23 (define): Pgvector/Shutterstock; 23 (ideate): Pgvector/Shutterstock; 23 (protoype): Pgvector/Shutterstock; 24 (left): PureSolution/Shutterstock; 24 (center left): PureSolution/Shutterstock; 24 (center right): PureSolution/Shutterstock; 24 (right): PureSolution/Shutterstock; 25: Metamorworks/Shutterstock; 27 (Louise): Fizkes/Shutterstock; 27 (Nick): Damir Khabirov/Shutterstock; 27 (Anita): AshTproductions/Shutterstock; 28 (top left): Dejan Bozic/123RF; 28 (top center): Dejan Bozic/123RF; 28 (top right): Dejan Bozic/123RF; 28 (bottom left): Dejan Bozic/123RF; 28 (bottom right): Dejan Bozic/123RF; 29: HAKINMHAN/Shutterstock; 31 (1): Wavebreakmedia/Shutterstock; 31 (2): Pheelings media/Shutterstock; 31 (3): DC Studio/Shutterstock; 31 (4): Fizkes/Shutterstock; 31 (5): Fizkes/Shutterstock; 32: Aleksandr Merg/Shutterstock; 33: Fizkes/Shutterstock; 35: Seanprai/Shutterstock; 37: Rawpixel.com/Shutterstock; 39 (1): Ivanko80/Shutterstock; 39 (2): Mangostar/Shutterstock; 39 (3): David Gyung/Shutterstock; 41: Jacob Lund/Shutterstock; 44: Colorlife/Shutterstock; 45: ImageFlow/Shutterstock; 47 (1, Purvi): Pressmaster/Shutterstock; 47 (2, Minato): Jacob Lund/Shutterstock; 47 (1, Brianna): Prostock-studio/Shutterstock; 47 (1, Joe): PH888/Shutterstock; 48: M.Style/Shutterstock; 49: George Rudy/Shutterstock; 51 (paper background): Natsukichi/Shutterstock; 51 (clipboard and pencil): Sumkinn/Shutterstock; 52: Natsukichi/Shutterstock; 74 (Judy avatar): B Studio And Design/Shutterstock; 74 (Pat avatar): B Studio And Design/Shutterstock; 75: Roman Sotola/Shutterstock; 76: Shutterstock; 77: Jesadaphorn chaiinkeaw/123RF; 77: Jesadaphorn chaiinkeaw/123RF; 78: Hermin/Shutterstock; 79 (woman avatar): Gurza/Shutterstock; 80: VectorsMarket/Shutterstock; 81 (woman and man avatars): Gurza/Shutterstock; 82 (woman and man avatars): Gurza/Shutterstock; 83: Singleline/Shutterstock; 84 (avatar): Kjpargeter/Shutterstock; 84 (avatar): Kjpargeter/Shutterstock; 84 (tablet frame): Alex_Murphy/Shutterstock.

Scope and Sequence

Welcome page 2	In the classroom | Learn about your book | Meet your Employability Skills Coaches

Module	I can . . .	Learning Objectives	Vocabulary
1 **Communication 1** Speaking Professionally pages 5–8	I can explain how to speak in a professional manner.	• Explain the importance of speaking professionally • Identify ways to sound more professional	*ample, approachable, commanding, condescending, conviction, convincingly, ensure, manner, merely, mumble*
2 **Communication 2** Developing Presentation Skills pages 9–12	I can explain how to prepare and deliver efficient presentations.	• Explain the importance of good presentation skills • Describe how to create effective presentations • Prepare to give presentations to an audience	*accomplished, anecdote, conversational, cram, lighten up, pitch, recap, rule of thumb, subordinate, wrap up*
3 **Goal Setting** Cascading Goals pages 13–16	I can explain the benefits of cascading a company's strategic goals.	• Describe the process of cascading goals • Describe the pros and cons of cascading goals • Explain the benefits of cascading goals for the company	*alignment, break down, bureaucratic, cascade, filter down, inspirational, keep track of, outdated, overload, performance, strategic, transparency*
4 **Teamwork** Remote Team Spirit pages 17–20	I can describe strategies to maintain team spirit in remote working.	• Describe the importance and benefits of maintaining the team spirit • Identify ways to build and maintain team spirit in remote working	*camaraderie, compensate, foster, frankly, guru, hybrid, isolated, remotely, underlying, utterly*
5 **Critical Thinking** Using Design Thinking pages 21–24	I can describe design thinking and how it works.	• Describe design thinking • Explain the benefits of solving problems with design thinking • Identify the steps of the design thinking process	*brainstorming, collaborative, empathize, immersion, insight, iteration, mainstream, multidisciplinary, prototype, refine, synthesize, unleash*
6 **Leadership** Change Leadership pages 25–28	I can describe change leadership and the characteristics of a good change leader.	• Explain the importance and benefits of change leadership • Describe the challenges of change leadership • Describe ways to be a good change leader	*advantageous, downsize, drum up, envision, implement, lay-off, morale, perseverance, resonate with, up-to-date*

Pronunciation	Language Strategy	Project	Talk!
Weak and blended pronunciation of *to*	Guess meaning from context	Interview someone who speaks with confidence	Common mistakes when trying to sound professional
Stressed and unstressed words	Understand colloquial language in presentations	Research tips on preparing effective presentations	Facts on presentation skills
Stress in phrasal verbs	Follow the sequence of arguments	Create an imaginary scenario with a cascading goal	Discuss the facts about companies that use the cascading goals strategy
Weak pronunciation of object pronouns	Infer meaning and attitude	Interview people about their remote working situations and how their companies have ensured a sense of teamwork	Facts about team spirit
Intonation to end or continue a thought	Understand explicit details and examples	Come up with improvements for a product or service using the design thinking process	Discuss statistics about companies that use design thinking
Stress with word endings	Infer the writer's attitude	Create an imaginary scenario where you implement a change to your company	Discuss research related to change leadership

Module	I can . . .	Learning Objectives	Vocabulary
7 **Self-Management** The Power of Mistakes pages 29–32	I can explain ways to adopt a growth mindset.	• Describe the importance of a growth mindset • Explain the benefits of having a growth mindset in the workplace	*consequential, discouraged, embrace, hypothesis, mindset, over and over, refute, simply, tenacity, vital*
8 **Wellness** Healthy Thinking pages 33–36	I can describe ways to maintain healthy thinking.	• Describe the importance and benefits of healthy thinking • Identify strategies and techniques for healthy thinking • Explain how to deal with challenges to healthy thinking	*cognitive, compassion, distorted, fall into the trap, jump to conclusions, mindful, misinterpret, obsess about, positively, psychologist, rationally, visualize*
9 **Social Responsibility** Assessing Cultural Differences pages 37–40	I can explain Hofstede's cultural dimensions.	• Describe challenges of culturally diverse workplaces • Use Hofstede's cultural dimensions to understand my colleagues from different cultures • Identify ways to avoid misunderstandings and overcome problems caused by cultural differences	*assertiveness, atypical, conversely, divergent, individualism, indulgent, persistence, restrained, sincerity, thrift*
10 **Branding** Personal Branding Mistakes pages 41–44	I can describe ways to avoid personal branding mistakes and strategies to fix mistakes if they occur.	• Detect common branding mistakes • Explain ways to avoid common branding mistakes • Explain how to repair and maintain a personal brand if mistakes are made	*capitalize on, cutting edge, deviate from, far-reaching, limitation, mismatch, pin the blame on, trait, trustworthy, vent*
11 **Job Search** Building Your Career pages 45–48	I can explain ways to build my career.	• State the importance of building my career • Describe ways to build my career	*aspire, caveat, finite, frustrated, proactive, recruiter, resilience, savvy, sponsor, trail off*
12 **Interviewing** Following up after an Interview pages 49–52	I can describe ways to follow up after a job interview.	• Explain the importance of following up after a job interview • Identify the proper ways to follow up after a job interview	*antagonistic, courtesy, digest, intense, job hunter, pest, prospect, pushy, threatening, vie, wordy*

Pronunciation	Language Strategy	Project	Talk!
Linking a vowel to a vowel	Recognize and evaluate the effectiveness of rhetorical devices in media presentations	Research the internet about different responses to mistakes	Discuss research about learning from mistakes
The sounds /ʃ/, /ʒ/, /tʃ/, /dʒ/	Identify key points in conceptual presentations (outside your field)	Choose a technique to improve your thinking habits	Discuss the quotes on healthy thinking
Consonant groups	Identify supporting examples in complex texts	Rate your cultural dimensions and compare with another country	Discuss the United States' score according to Hofstede's Cultural Dimensions
The letter *a*	Recognize summarizing expressions	Interview someone about their personal brand	Common personal branding mistakes
The sounds /u/, /ʊ/, and /ʌ/	Follow a panel discussion on complex, unfamiliar topics	Identify skills to develop	Discuss statistics about career development
Thought groups	Follow the flow of dialogue in complex discussions	Interview someone who recruits or who got a job in the past few years	Common mistakes job seekers make when following-up after an interview

To the Teacher

Overview

Step Up is a flexible online course designed for adults or young adults who want to improve their employability skills—whether to get a first job, secure a promotion, find a different job, re-enter the workforce after an absence, or change fields. Although the emphasis of the course is on employability skills, *Step Up* also develops English language skills by providing vocabulary instruction and practice, listening, reading, and notetaking skills, pronunciation practice, and discussion strategies.

Levels

There are six levels of *Step Up*, CEFR A2+ to C1, Global Scale of English (GSE) 34 to 84.

***Step Up* level**	**GSE**
Step Up A2+	34–43
Step Up B1	41–51
Step Up B1+	49–58
Step Up B2	56–66
Step Up B2+	64–75
Step Up C1	73–84

Two Versions of *Step Up*

Students can study the *Step Up* course in two ways: as a self-study course or as a self-study plus course, which is the self-study course combined with a teacher-led class. As a self-study course, each level of *Step Up* takes students 18 hours to complete, though this may vary as it is self-paced. The teacher-led course provides 14 hours of class time, with additional resources and extension activities available in the Teaching Notes, which would extend class time.

Student's Components

	Self-study course	**Self-study plus course**
Online Course	✓	✓
Coursebook + eBook or eBook only	✗	✓
Resources (online)	✓	✓

Teacher's Components

	Self-study plus course
Coursebook and/or eBook	✓
Access to the Online Course	✓
Teaching Notes	✓
Resources (online)	✓

The Online Course

Students study the following 12 modules, of which the first nine are **personal and social capabilities** and the last three are job-seeking skills:

Module 1 Communication 1	**Module 2** Communication 2	**Module 3** Goal Setting
Module 4 Teamwork	**Module 5** Critical Thinking	**Module 6** Leadership
Module 7 Self-Management	**Module 8** Wellness	**Module 9** Social Responsibility
Module 10 Branding	**Module 11** Job Search	**Module 12** Interviewing

Each module has an employability skills coach—an animated character—who takes the students through the 10 steps of the module. Step 11 is a progress check; it includes a practice test and a graded test. If the student scores at least 70% on every graded test, they are given access to the final exam. If they score at least 80% on this assessment, they receive a certificate of completion.

For a closer look at the online course, please see the Online Module Walkthrough in the Teacher Resources.

Coursebook/eBook

The Coursebook/eBook is made up of two main sections: the modules and the back matter.

The Modules

Welcome module

The Coursebook begins with a Welcome module, which is comprised of four sections to:

- help students get to know each other and form a community of learners
- provide students with useful language they need to work effectively in class
- help students navigate the Coursebook so they get the most out of it
- introduce students to the 12 employability skills coaches they meet in the online course.

The 12 Employability Skills Modules

Following the Welcome module are the 12 employability skills modules, corresponding to each module in the online course. Students need to do each online module before they come to class. In class, you guide them through each module to reinforce what they have learned online, to deepen their understanding of the material, and to share how they can apply what they have learned to their own lives.

Back Matter

There are four sections in the back of the Coursebook and eBook:

- *Check your understanding* enables students to demonstrate they have understood the material they have studied online and gives them an opportunity to clear up any misunderstandings at the beginning of a class.
- *Discussion strategies* provide students with four different sets of strategies that can help them engage in class. These include how to work with others; clarify what you hear or clarify what you say; get and stay involved in the discussion; and organize your ideas. Audio models enable students to practice their pronunciation.
- *Vocabulary practice* gives students additional practice with the vocabulary they have learned in the online course. The first activity is a word puzzle, and the second activity uses the target words from the puzzle in context. The answers are provided in the eBook and in the Resources folder.
- *The Glossary* provides the definitions of some words or phrases printed in light brown in the Coursebook to facilitate understanding.

Flexibility

While the sequence of the modules is fixed in the coursebook, you can change the sequence to meet the needs of your students. You may want to have the class review the scope and sequence and vote on which modules to do first. If you change the sequence, we suggest you create a syllabus and upload it to the platform.

Resources for Students

All audio and video files for the online course and all audio files for the coursebook are accessible within the activities in the course. In addition, these audio and video files are also available in the Resources, to allow students to watch or listen whenever they wish without going to the lesson itself. Also included in the Resources are the reading texts, as well as answer keys to the *Vocabulary practice* in the Coursebook.

Resources for Teachers

Teaching Notes

There are general teaching notes to help you get the most out of the course. Then there are notes for each module that begin with an overview of the online module that synopsizes what the students have learned online. Following the overview are teaching notes for each step in the coursebook, including tips, extensions, culture notes, and more.

Module Walkthrough

There is also a module walkthrough that visually describes a module and the underlying pedagogy for both the online course and the coursebook.

Platform Support

To help you navigate the platform and use all the tools available, there is a guided tour when you first log on to Pearson English Connect. In addition, you will find numerous resources under the "Help" button to orient you to the platform. And to get in touch with support, you can click on Help>Documentation>Contact Support.

Welcome

① In the classroom

A Get to know your classmates

Talk to your classmates. Find someone who matches each prompt. Write their first name on the line. Then ask follow-up questions.

- enjoys shopping ____________
- loves scary movies ____________
- is afraid of heights ____________
- can draw ____________
- has traveled to another country ____________
- is very athletic ____________

B Useful language

Here are some examples of strategies that will help you overcome challenges in discussions with classmates or colleagues. Complete the tips with the problems in the box. Then listen and choose the strategies that you hear.

a ~~doesn't participate~~	**d** speaks too much
b speaks too quickly	**e** speaks too softly
c goes off topic	**f** interrupts others

☐ **1** If someone doesn't participate, invite him or her to join in by saying things like …
- "What do you think, Diego?"
- "We haven't heard from Chiyo yet. What do you think about …?"

☐ **2** If someone ____________, get him or her back on track by saying things like …
- "Let's return to what Lanh was saying."
- "That's a good point, but let's get back to the main issue."

☐ **3** If someone is impatient and frequently ____________, you can say …
- "Wait your turn, please. You'll have a chance to talk in a moment."
- "Hold on. Let Malik finish what he's saying."

☐ **4** If someone ____________ and others don't have the opportunity to speak, you can politely interrupt by saying …
- "Thank you, Noor. Now let's hear what other people have to say."
- "That's an interesting idea. What do you think about that, Jae-jin?"

☐ **5** If someone ____________, ask him or her to slow down by saying …
- "Would you mind slowing down?"
- "Could you say that a little more slowly, please?"

☐ **6** If someone ____________, and others have trouble understanding what is being said, get him or her to speak up by saying …
- "Would you mind speaking up a little?"
- "I'm afraid we can't hear what you're saying."

C Discuss

GROUPS **Discuss the strategies in 1B. Which ones are the most/least useful? Say why.**

② Learn about your book

1 How many modules are in the course?

a 5 **b** 9 **c** 11 **d** 12

2 How many steps are in each module?

a 6 **b** 7 **c** 8 **d** 9

3 Look at this icon on page 5.
It tells you to go to page 68.
Read what is on that page.
How can you use that
information?

DISCUSSION STRATEGIES

Go to page 68.

____

4 On page 5, Exercise C says Check your understanding. Go to page 54. What is on that page?

a questions to test vocabulary
b questions to ask my teacher
c questions to review the Online Course
d questions to ask my partner

5 Look through Module 1. Which Steps in the book refer to Steps in the Online Course?

a Steps 1, 2, and 3
b Steps 2, 5, and 7
c Steps 3, 4, and 6
d Steps 5, 6, and 7

6 Look at the I-can statement after Step 7 in each module, for example

I can identify successful communication skills. ☐

What is it for?

____

7 What will you find on pages 74–85?

a listening practice
b grammar practice
c vocabulary practice
d pronunciation practice

8 What will you find on pages 86–87?

a a glossary
b listening activities
c vocabulary practice
d an audio script

To find the answers for CHECK YOUR UNDERSTANDING and VOCABULARY PRACTICE you can look in your ebook or use the answer key in the Student's Resources online.

Meet your Employability Skills Coaches

MODULE 1
Greetings! I'm Dr. Jabu Cele. I have my doctorate in communications and I'm a senior vice president at one of the world's top marketing companies.

MODULE 2
Hi there! I'm Emma Lu, and I'll be your coach for the Communication 2 module. I'm a corporate teamwork coach.

MODULE 3
Hello there. I'm Zehra Teke and I'll be your Employability Skills coach for the module about Goal Setting. I'm a business consultant with a master's degree in management.

MODULE 4
Hello! My name is Kristine Ross. I'm the human resources manager for a large, international company. I'll be your coach for the Teamwork module.

MODULE 5
Hello. My name is Marek Kamiński. I'm an investigative journalist and I'll be your Employability Skills coach for the Critical Thinking module.

MODULE 6
Hi, I'm Sonia Lopez. I'll be your coach for the Leadership module. I'm the Chief Executive Officer—the CEO—of the Alacarte Restaurant Group.

MODULE 7
Hello, my name is Felix Becker. I'm a professional certified life coach and I'll be your coach for the Self-Management module.

MODULE 8
Hello and welcome to the Wellness module. I'll be your Employability Skills coach. My name is Kai Sugimoto. I have a PhD in psychology and I do research on health and wellness.

MODULE 9
Hello, there. My name is Ana Silva. I'm the coordinator of social responsibilty for a large company and I am your coach for the Social Responsibilty module.

MODULE 10
Hi. Welcome to the Branding module. I'm Rakesh Patel, and I'm your Employability Skills coach. I work in marketing.

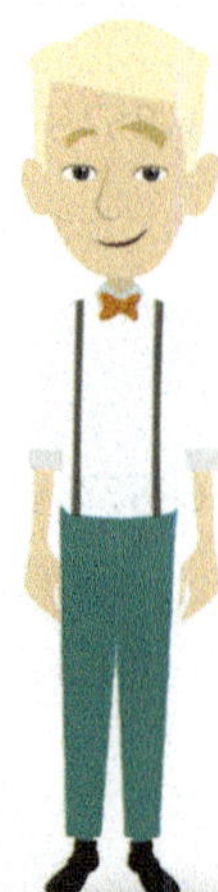

MODULE 11
Hello! Welcome. I'm Justin Roy, and I'm your coach for the Job Search module. I'm a career advice blogger and my goal is to help people find their dream jobs.

MODULE 12
Hi. My name is Aisha Omar. I'm a career counselor at the U.S. Department of Labor and I'll be your coach for the Interviewing module.

1

MODULE

Communication 1

Speaking Professionally

DISCUSSION STRATEGIES

Go to page 68.

Step 1 Get started

A Refresh your memory! Watch the *What You'll Learn* video.

B Look at the photo below. Are these co-workers communicating with each other in a professional manner? Explain.

C Check your understanding. Go to page 54.

Step ② Tell your story

A THINK In your online course, you thought about a time when the tone you or someone else used caused a problem or a miscommunication. What happened and how did you proceed? Listen to the example.

B PAIRS Discuss your story.

C SHARE Tell your story to the class.

Step ③ Take away

A PAIRS Review your notes from the online module and complete the chart.

Appropriate tone of voice can ...	Striking the wrong tone can result in ...
✓ ______________________	✓ ______________________
✓ ______________________	✓ ______________________
✓ ______________________	✓ ______________________
To feel and sound confident ...	
Before Speaking	During Speaking
✓ ______________________	✓ ______________________
✓ ______________________	✓ ______________________
✓ ______________________	✓ ______________________
✓ ______________________	✓ ______________________

B SHARE Compare your chart with another pair's. What can you add to your chart?

Step 4 Activate your knowledge

A PAIRS Listen to the conversations. Discuss each person's tone. What problems do you hear? What can the speakers do to sound more professional?

1 OSCAR

Oscar is meeting a new co-worker for the first time. Listen to their conversation. What can Oscar do to sound more professional?

2 KENT

Kent is giving his co-worker information about an upcoming conference. Listen to their conversation. What can Kent do to sound more professional?

3 SHIVAYA

Shivaya's manager is giving her feedback on some reports she recently submitted. Listen to their conversation. What can Shivaya do to sound more professional?

4 ROSA

Rosa and her co-worker have been assigned to work on a project together. Listen to their conversation. What can Rosa do to sound more professional?

B PAIRS Choose two situations from A. Role-play them. Make sure to use professional tone.

C SHARE Share your experience with the class. Explain the strategies you used for speaking with a more professional tone of voice.

Step 5 Project

A PAIRS In your online course, you interviewed someone who speaks with confidence, conviction, and the right emotional tone. Tell your partner about your interview. Read the example.

I interviewed a colleague who does a lot of presenting for our company. He told me that he sometimes gets really nervous, even though he's done it a lot! But he has specific things that he does to prepare ahead of time. He said he practices a lot at home, first by himself, then in front of his family. Right before the presentation, he does some breathing exercises so that he stays calm. As far as unexpected questions, he said that he tries to anticipate people's questions so that he won't get surprised. But if he does, he takes a deep breath and thinks for a minute before answering.

B SHARE Share your interview with the class.

Step 6 Talk!

PAIRS Read some common mistakes that could prevent you from sounding professional. Rank them from 1 (most serious) to 8 (least serious). Explain your reasons.

- ☐ Responding immediately when you are emotional
- ☐ Speaking too quickly or too slowly
- ☐ Using a lot of fillers
- ☐ Speaking too loudly or too softly
- ☐ Being very sarcastic
- ☐ Using flat intonation
- ☐ Speak without confidence
- ☐ Sounding negative

Step 7 Going forward

A PAIRS In your online course, you reflected on how you could develop your skills in speaking professionally after studying more about it. Discuss. Listen to the example.

B SHARE Present your ideas to the class.

VOCABULARY PRACTICE
Go to page 74.

I can explain how to speak in a professional manner. ☐

2 MODULE

Communication 2

Developing Presentation Skills

DISCUSSION STRATEGIES

Go to page 68.

Step ① Get started

A Refresh your memory! Watch the *What You'll Learn* video.

B Look at the photo. Does the presenter seem to be making their presentation effectively? Why?

C Check your understanding. Go to page 55.

Step ② Tell your story

A THINK In your online course, you thought about a time when you prepared a presentation. Was it an effective presentation? Why? Why not? Listen to the example.

B PAIRS Discuss your story.

C SHARE Tell your story to the class.

Step ③ Take away

A THINK Review your notes from the online module. Match the questions with the presentation aspects they describe.

Preparing and Giving Effective Presentations	
____ 1. What technology will you need?	a. the purpose/aim of your presentation
____ 2. How will you engage the audience and lighten up the presentation?	b. the audience
____ 3. How long will it last?	c. audience involvement
____ 4. How will you stress an important point?	d. timing
____ 5. Why are you giving the presentation?	e. equipment
____ 6. Will they be the main focus, or will they just underline what you are saying?	f. purpose of slides
____ 7. Will there be only text or mostly images?	g. content of slides
____ 8. Who is the presentation for and how much do they know?	h. design of slides
____ 9. Will you accept questions from the audience during or after your presentation?	i. use of anecdotes, questions, humor
____ 10. Which font, point size, images, animation will you use?	j. changes in volume or pitch and use of gestures, body language

B PAIRS Check your answers with a partner.

Step 4 Activate your knowledge

A THINK Linda is giving a presentation. Look at the slides and listen to this short presentation. Use the questions below as a guide. Take notes.

How to Evaluate Information

Linda Rogers

Tips for Evaluating Information

Don't take information at face value. Ask yourself:

- Is the source credible? Is the speaker or author trustworthy? Is he or she an authority on the subject? Does he or she cite sources?
- Is the language objective or emotional? Does the speaker or author use absolute language?
- Are there problems with the logic? Does the speaker or author try to make things seem equal when they're not? Do claims fall apart when you think about them more carefully?

1. What is the purpose of this presentation?

   ____

2. Who is the intended audience?

   ____

3. What does the presenter do well?

   ____

4. What could the presenter improve on?

   ____

B PAIRS Discuss your notes with a partner. Then help Linda improve her presentation. How can she improve her slides, language, and delivery?

C SHARE Share your ideas with the class.

Step 5 Project

A PAIRS In your online course, you did research on useful tips to help you prepare effective presentations. Share your favorite. Read the example.

I found a tip about the importance of the beginning of the presentation. I believe it's crucial to start the presentation by grabbing the audience's attention. Effective openers include things like beginning with an entertaining anecdote or an intriguing image, asking a thought-provoking question, stating a shocking statistic, or using a powerful quote. These kinds of attention-getting openers help speakers engage the audience from the start, and they have the added benefit of familiarizing them with the topic and motivating them to listen.

B SHARE Share your tips with the class.

Step 6 Talk!

PAIRS Presentation skills are considered to be a key to career success. Read the facts and then discuss the questions.

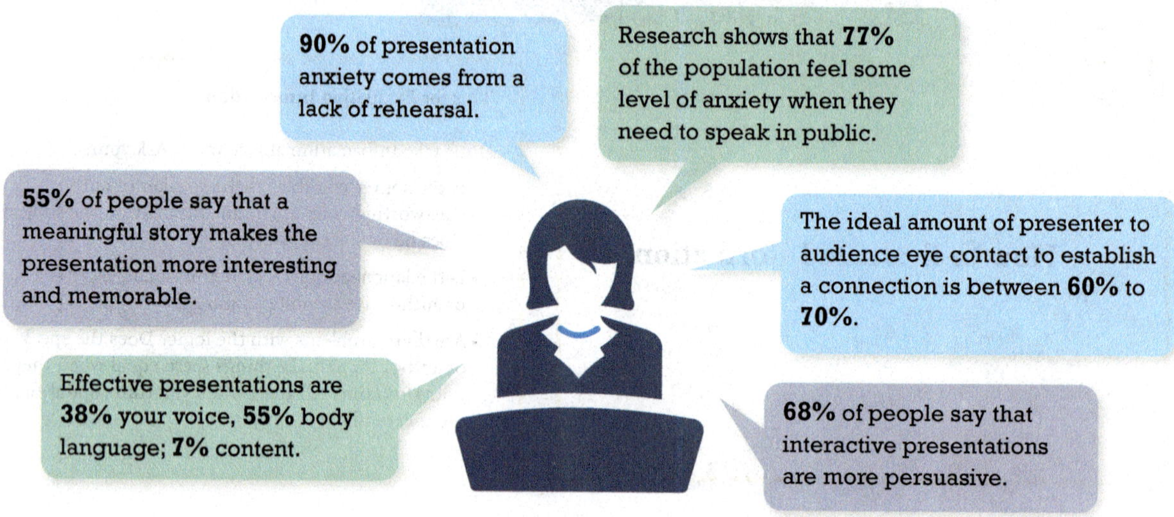

- Are any of these facts surprising to you? Why?
- Why do you think presentation skills are so important in the workplace?
- Which one of these facts do you think is the most important?

Step 7 Going forward

A PAIRS In your online course, you reflected on how you could develop your presentation skills after studying more about it. Discuss. Listen to the example.

B SHARE Present your ideas to the class.

VOCABULARY PRACTICE
Go to page 75.

I can explain how to prepare and deliver effective presentations. ☐

3
MODULE

Goal Setting

Cascading Goals

DISCUSSION STRATEGIES

Go to page 68.

Step ① Get started

A Refresh your memory! Watch the *What You'll Learn* video.

B Look at the photo. Is it related to the idea of cascading goals? Why or why not? How is it related to cascading goals? Why are cascading goals good for everyone in the company?

C Check your understanding. Go to page 56.

Step ② Tell your story

A THINK In your online course, you thought about the importance of cascading goals. Did you know what your employer's goals were? If so, how did you know? Were those goals met? If not, how did not knowing your employer's goals impact you? Listen to the example.

B PAIRS Discuss your story.

C SHARE Tell your story to the class.

Step ③ Take away

A PAIRS Use your notes from the online module. Complete the chart with words from the box.

achieve	alignment	conflicting	method	misunderstandings	
performance	review	reward	track	time-consuming	transparency

SETTING CASCADING GOALS

Purpose:

- To create [1]__________ between the company's strategy and the work at every part of the business.

Benefits:

- Provides [2]__________ about company strategy.
- Makes clear what the company aims to [3]__________.
- Makes it easier to [4]__________ objectives and [5]__________ progress.
- Generates greater levels of effort and [6]__________.

Pitfalls:

- Process could be slow, [7]__________, or bureaucratic.
- Poor communication or vague goals can result in [8]__________, misalignment of objectives, [9]__________ goals, duplication of work, and inefficiencies.

Tips:

- Use of the SMART [10]__________ to set goals.
- Provide necessary support or resources, [11]__________ the achievements.

B SHARE Compare your answers with the class.

Step ④ Activate your knowledge

A GROUPS Imagine that you are executives at Novel-Tee, a company that sells graphic T-shirts. You have decided to use a cascading goal framework throughout your organization. Look at the chart below. Discuss how each business level aligns with the business strategy. Take notes in the chart.

Novel-Tee Business Strategy: Increase T-shirt sales in existing markets by 30% by the end of the year.

Business level	Goals	Alignment
Department: Product design	Produce 20 new T-shirt designs in each of five key markets for a total of 100 new designs by the end of year.	
Team: Souvenirs	Produce 5 new souvenir T-shirt designs each quarter for popular tourist destinations, for a total of 20 new designs by the end of the year.	
Individual: Designer	In the next three months, produce 3–5 new designs for souvenir T-shirts for adults visiting Bogotá.	

B GROUPS Make a plan for putting cascading goals into practice. Think about how you will avoid common pitfalls. Use the questions below to guide your discussion.

1. How will you ensure that goals filter down to every level of the business?

2. How will you communicate with different business levels?

3. How will you ensure that the process is quick and flexible?

4. How will you ensure that employees remain motivated and engaged?

5. How will you monitor the performance of the employees and teams?

C SHARE Share your plan with the class.

Step 5 Project

A PAIRS In your online course, you created an imaginary scenario where you set a cascading goal. Tell your partner about it. Read the example.

The cascading goal I set for the company I'd like to work for is to attract 10,000 visitors to a website that promotes a new product over the next three months. I would announce the goal in a meeting with the middle management team. Each department would think of strategies to help achieve it. For instance, the marketing team might decide to have a big email campaign to reach out to our old customers. The sales team might suggest offering discounts to get the attention of new customers. The production team might devise a short YouTube video about the product that would redirect viewers to the website. Supervisors would check each team's progress and monitor results weekly and then report to their managers.

B SHARE Share your scenario with the class.

Step 6 Talk!

PAIRS Read these facts about companies that use the cascading goals strategy. Then discuss the questions.

30% higher levels of innovation

40% higher levels of employee retention

73% communicate goals more formally

73% of employees feel more engaged

- How might cascading goals contribute to innovation?
- Why do you think employees are more likely to continue working for companies with cascading goals?
- What are the different ways that companies might formally communicate their goals?
- Are you surprised by how many employees feel more engaged by cascading goals? Why or why not?

Step 7 Going forward

A PAIRS In your online course, you reflected on how you could improve your skills in setting effective cascading goals after studying more about it. Discuss. Listen to the example.

B SHARE Present your ideas to the class.

VOCABULARY PRACTICE Go to page 76.

I can explain the benefits of cascading a company's strategic goals. ☐

4
MODULE

Teamwork

Remote Team Spirit

DISCUSSION STRATEGIES

Go to page 68.

Step 1 Get started

A Refresh your memory! Watch the *What You'll Learn* video.

B Look at the photo. How is it related to working remotely? Do you think it's a successful strategy? Explain.

C Check your understanding. Go to page 57.

Step ② Tell your story

A THINK In your online course, you thought about a time that you or someone you know worked remotely. Did it affect your sense of team spirit? If so, how? Listen to the example.

B PAIRS Discuss your story.

C SHARE Tell your story to the class.

Step ③ Take away

A PAIRS Review your notes from the online module and complete the sentences with your ideas.

To build and maintain team spirit in remote and hybrid work situations:		
Videoconferencing	**Status meetings**	**Team-building activities**
• Potential problems are: ______ ______ ______	• Advantages to remote teams: ______ ______ ______ ______ ______ ______ ______	• These activities should be: ______ ______ ______ ______ ______ ______ ______
• Possible solutions are: ______ ______ ______		

B SHARE Compare your ideas with the class.

Step ④ Activate your knowledge

A PAIRS Read about these teams and their problems. Then discuss the questions.

1

ASTRID

I am a product manager at a small technology company. Upper management recently announced plans to transition from working in an office to working remotely. At the start of the next quarter, all staff are expected to work from home instead of coming into the office. While some people are looking forward to the change because they prefer working from home, others—like me—are a little worried about the change. For example, my team has weekly meetings to discuss our projects. Without being able to meet in person, I'm concerned that the team will be less productive, and that teamwork and camaraderie will suffer.

1. Why is it important for Astrid's team to maintain team spirit while working remotely?
______
2. What are some challenges that she might face when the team transitions to remote work?
______

2

STERLING

I lead a research team at a medical device company. On our team, we have a mix of on-site, remote, and hybrid workers. Every Monday, we have a status meeting. Some people attend the meeting in person, while others call in. This arrangement has worked well in the past, but recently, there have been some problems. A few remote workers have complained that they feel left out during meetings. They say that the on-site employees do all the talking while the remote employees don't get a chance to say anything. I want to make sure that everyone feels included and involved but, frankly, I'm not sure how to do that.

1. Why is it important for Sterling to address the remote employees' concerns?

2. What are some challenges that he might face in addressing employees' concerns?

3

CAMILA

I manage my company's data analysis department. Our group has been fully remote for about six months. So far, we have maintained a high level of team spirit and productivity. Recently, I hired a new analyst. He is the first person to join the team since we transitioned to remote work. The rest of us have worked together in person before, but the new employee won't have that opportunity. I want to make him feel welcome and like he's part of the team, but I'm not sure how to do that with everyone working remotely.

1. Why is it important for Camila to make sure that the new employee feels like part of the team?

2. What are some challenges that she might face in making the new employee feel like part of the team?

B GROUPS of 3–5 **Discuss steps that each person can take to build and maintain team spirit on their team. Create a plan for each one.**

C SHARE **Present your plan to another group.**

Step 5 Project

A PAIRS In your online course, you interviewed people about their remote working situations, and what their companies have done to ensure a sense of teamwork. Tell your partner what you learned. Read the example.

One friend I interviewed has a fully remote setup because her company hires people from all over the world. They've had to be really creative in figuring out how to make everyone feel like they're part of the same team—while living in different time zones, too! They have weekly status meetings, scheduled at a convenient time for everyone, and they rotate the task of preparing minutes so no single person gets overwhelmed. But the most interesting thing they've done is set up online social spaces with activities and games for the team to play together. Of course, it's totally optional, but my friend said they are so fun, everyone does them. They've learned a lot about each other that way, and they really feel like part of a team.

B SHARE Discuss your findings with the class.

Step 6 Talk!

PAIRS Read the facts about team spirit. For each fact, say whether or not it surprises you, and then explain why you agree with them.

54% of employees say that a sense of team spirit motivates them to work at the same company longer.

Feelings of isolation among employees reduces productivity up to 21%.

33% of human resources specialists report that poor team collaboration leads to low employee morale.

56% of employers say that they are using online collaboration tools to maintain team spirit.

Team spirit can increase successful innovation by 15%.

64% of employees say that they stay more committed to their tasks and goals when there is collaboration.

Step 7 Going forward

A PAIRS In your online course, you reflected on how you approach remote work differently to maintain team spirit after studying more about it. Discuss. Listen to the example.

B SHARE Present your ideas to the class.

VOCABULARY PRACTICE
Go to page 77.

I can describe strategies to maintain team spirit in remote working. ☐

MODULE 5

Critical Thinking

Using Design Thinking

DISCUSSION STRATEGIES

Go to page 68.

Step 1 Get started

A Refresh your memory! Watch the *What You'll Learn* video.

B Look at the photo. How is this team using design thinking? Explain.

C Check your understanding. Go to page 58.

Step 2 Tell your story

A THINK In your online course, you thought about a time when you noticed an improvement to a product you use that you think may have been the result of design thinking. Listen to the example.

B PAIRS Discuss your story.

C SHARE Tell your story to the class.

Step 3 Take away

A PAIRS Use your notes from the online module. Complete the statements about the five stages of design thinking.

convergent	refine	pain points	feedback
choose	unmet needs	reactions	generate

The Five Stages of Design Thinking

Stage 1: Empathize

- Research and discover your users' [1] ____________________

Stage 2: Define

- Write a problem statement: Reflect the customers' [2] ____________________

Stage 3: Ideate

- [3] ____________________ ideas e.g., brainstorming technique (divergent to [4] ____________________ thinking)

Stage 4: Prototype

- [5] ____________________ the best possible solution
- Test it and get [6] ____________________ from customers

Stage 5: Test

- Try your solutions out and observe users' [7] ____________________
- Ask follow-up questions
- [8] ____________________ the product or service before implementation

B GROUPS Compare your answers with the class. Can you add more ideas?

Step ④ Activate your knowledge

A PAIRS **Imagine that you work at a local bank. You want to encourage people to open bank accounts. You decide to use design thinking to create a product that will attract customers. Read each stage of the design thinking process. Then apply them to your product.**

Empathize

Interview your partner about his or her experience with banking. Use the following questions as a guide. Remember to ask follow-up questions.

1 What is your experience with banking?

2 What do you do at your bank?

3 Are you happy with your bank? Why or why not?

____

____

Define

Compare your answers from the *empathize* stage to find common issues. Then write a problem statement that includes the background and the desired outcome. Remember to use action verbs.

____

____

Ideate

Spend five minutes brainstorming product ideas individually. Then discuss your ideas with your partner.

____

____

Prototype

Select one or two product ideas from the *ideate* stage. Make a thumbnail sketch that shows your idea.

Test

Share your idea and your thumbnail sketch with another pair. Ask for feedback about your product idea.

____

____

B SHARE **Share your ideas with the class. Describe how the design thinking process helped you to come up with your product.**

Step 5 Project

A PAIRS **In your online course, you followed the design thinking process to come up with improvements for a product or service. What product or service did you choose to improve and how? Tell your partner about it. Read the example.**

I'm a developer at a video streaming service. I worked with my colleagues to learn about users' experiences with our service. We prepared a list of questions about how people interact with the app once they've opened it. Through our survey, we learned that people love our "recommended" section, but if they want to try something completely different, they have a hard time navigating to where they can browse by category. So we've developed some ideas for a better menu on the home screen which we hope to begin testing in a few weeks.

B SHARE **Discuss your findings with the class.**

Step 6 Talk!

PAIRS **Read these statistics about companies that use design thinking. Do they surprise you? Why or why not? Discuss explanations for each statistic.**

Step 7 Going forward

A PAIRS **In your online course, you reflected on how you apply design thinking to solve a problem at work or at home. Discuss. Listen to the example.**

B SHARE **Present your ideas to the class.**

VOCABULARY PRACTICE Go to page 78.

I can describe design thinking and how it works. ☐

6

MODULE

Leadership

Change Leadership

DISCUSSION STRATEGIES

Go to page 68.

Step 1

Get started

A Refresh your memory! Watch the *What You'll Learn* video.

B Look at the photo. How can this photo be related to change leadership? What do you think the change leader is thinking about?

C Check your understanding. Go to page 59.

Step 2 Tell your story

A THINK In your online course, you thought about a big change in your workplace. Did your company exhibit qualities of change leadership or not? How did this affect how well the change was implemented? Listen to the example.

B PAIRS Discuss your story.

C SHARE Tell your story to the class.

Step 3 Take away

A PAIRS Review your notes from the online module. Complete the sentences with your ideas.

A successful change leader must ...

- believe in the change vision and be enthusiastic about it.
  WHY?
  1 ______________________________
- look out for the well-being of the employees.
  HOW?
  By 2 ______________________ and ______________________
- develop 3 ______________________ and ______________________ strategies
- be ready to face challenges,
  such as 4 ______________________ and ______________________
- maintain morale during the change.
  HOW?
  By 5 ______________________________
  ____
  ____

B SHARE Compare your answers with the class.

Step 4 Activate your knowledge

A PAIRS Read and discuss each of the change scenarios below. Then answer the questions.

1. Why is a change leader important in each situation?
2. What are the benefits of change leadership in each scenario?
3. What challenges and difficult decisions will each change leader face?

LOUISE I am the Editorial Director for a small, independent news website. We publish articles about the environment and sustainability initiatives. The people on my staff are very passionate about our mission, and our site has a distinctive brand. Our publication was recently sold to a large media corporation that owns several newspapers, magazines, and news blogs. The staff is worried that the large company will push us to change our brand and that we will have less freedom to choose what to publish.

NICK I co-own a small construction company that was founded about 12 years ago. We've been very successful and our company has grown rapidly. As we hire more people, it is important that we think carefully about the direction in which our company grows. We have decided to develop and implement a Diversity and Inclusion (D&I) plan to make sure that we are attracting employees from different cultures and creating an atmosphere where all employees feel welcome. We are not sure about how to implement a D&I program. We are worried that some of our current employees will be resistant to changes in ways of doing things.

ANITA I run a small a non-profit organization that provides various services to people in our local community. We have a small staff—about 20 people—and we have developed a strong client base. Unfortunately, due to the recent economic downturn, our funding has been reduced. We need to find a way to save some money, but we already operate on a shoestring budget. I'm afraid that we'll have to reduce services or lay off staff.

B PAIRS Discuss how each person can be a change leader.

1. What are some strategies that they can implement?
2. How can they support employees and improve morale?
3. How can change leaders employ the three Cs?

C SHARE Present your ideas to the class.

Step 5 Project

A PAIRS In your online course, you created an imaginary scenario where you thought about a change your company would implement. Tell your partner about it. Read the example.

We sell home goods, both in-store and online. Normally, we just sell the products and, if needed, deliver them. My idea is to customize solutions for our customers by offering home visits before they buy something. We can assess their needs and offer solutions. We could also offer more services after a purchase, like building and installation. To offer these, we'd need to hire more workers. To be able to afford them, we might need to let some in-store salespeople go—if we can't re-train them for the new positions. Layoffs would be hard, but I think it would be easy enough to persuade those who are staying that this is good for all of us. They would gain new skills, and the business would be more competitive.

B SHARE Share your scenario with the class.

Step 6 Talk!

PAIRS Read the research related to change leadership and discuss the questions.

When employees are engaged in an organizational change, the success of the transformation increases by 71%.

69% of successfully implemented change programs have offered trainings to their employees both before and after the changes happen.

Less than 10% of leaders have the capability to manage an organizational change successfully.

Effective change leadership can increase employees' engagement by 45%.

Only 39% of participants say they have been involved in or inspired by an organizational change.

- Are any of these facts surprising to you? Which ones? Why?
- Why do you think that the percentage of leaders who can implement an organizational change successfully is so low? How can this be improved?
- Why do you think it is important to engage and inspire employees during periods of transformation? How can this be achieved?

Step 7 Going forward

A PAIRS In your online course, you reflected on how you can use the concepts of change leadership to inspire and implement change at your workplace. Discuss. Listen to the example.

B SHARE Present your ideas to the class.

VOCABULARY PRACTICE
Go to page 79.

I can describe change leadership and the characteristics of a good change leader. ☐

MODULE 7

Self-Management

The Power of Mistakes

DISCUSSION STRATEGIES
Go to page 68.

Step 1 Get started

A Refresh your memory! Watch the *What You'll Learn* video.

B Look at the photo. How is this photo related to learning from mistakes? What does it mean to you?

C Check your understanding. Go to page 60.

Step 2 Tell your story

A THINK In your online course, you thought about a time when you repeatedly made a mistake in your personal or professional life. How did you manage to avoid it? What did you do? Listen to the example.

B PAIRS Discuss your story.

C SHARE Tell your story to the class.

Step 3 Take away

A PAIRS Use your notes from the online module. Complete the sentences with your ideas.

People with a growth mindset . . .

1. believe that intelligence and abilities __________
2. see mistakes as __________
3. respond to mistakes with __________
4. __________ challenges.
5. see failure as a sign for them to __________
6. are more likely to __________

B SHARE Compare your answers with the class. Can you add more to the list?

Step ④ Activate your knowledge

A PAIRS For each *failure* in the chart, write a statement that shows a growth mindset.

Failure		Growth mindset
1 Lost a sports contest		*I should ask my coach for advice about my training so that I can do better in the next match.*
2 Got a bad grade on a test		
3 Didn't understand a project at work		
4 Got a bad performance review at work		
5 Was rejected for a job or promotion		

B PAIRS Share your *growth mindset* statement and compare them. Decide whose *growth mindset* statement is the more helpful. Give reasons.

C PAIRS Choose one of the *failures* above and write a *growth mindset* plan for responding. Use the questions below as a guide.

1. Why is a *growth mindset* important in this situation?
2. What questions can I ask myself in this situation?
3. What steps can I take to do better next time?

D SHARE Present your ideas to the class.

Step 5 Project

A PAIRS In your online course, you searched on the Internet and took notes about different responses to mistakes. Share them with your partner. Read the example.

I've read a few articles on the Internet about the way people deal with their emotions after having made a mistake. It's Ok to get frustrated or upset. I liked the strategy of letting ourselves feel those emotions. Instead of pushing aside our anxiety or anger, it's advised to find ways to release the tension. Apart from going for a run or taking a walk, screaming, or even laughing hysterically are suggested. Also, in order to get rid of negative thoughts, it is recommended to keep in mind that the mistakes we made do not define who we are as a person.

B SHARE Share your notes with the class.

Step 6 Talk!

PAIRS Learning from our mistakes and not being afraid of making them in the first place, can help us to fulfill our potential. Read the research. Does anything surprise you? Does the research align with your experiences? Explain.

Supportive and friendly work environments make it possible for employees to learn from their mistakes, whereas stressful and intolerant environments prevent employees from accepting their mistakes and learning from them.

40% of employees hold back because of their fear of failure.

Employees' self-motivation is positively associated with learning from mistakes and failures. In other words, the more we learn from our mistakes, the more motivated we become.

Research shows that if a task is too easy or too difficult, we don't learn. We learn the most if we fail 15% of the time and are successful the remaining 85% of the time.

Step 7 Going forward

A PAIRS In your online course, you reflected about adopting a growth mindset after studying more about the power of mistakes. Discuss. Listen to the example.

B SHARE Present your ideas to the class.

VOCABULARY PRACTICE
Go to page 80.

I can explain ways to adopt a growth mindset. ☐

MODULE 8

Wellness

Healthy Thinking

DISCUSSION STRATEGIES

Go to page 68.

Step 1 Get started

A Refresh your memory! Watch the *What You'll Learn* video.

B Look at the photo. What do you think the woman is doing? How do you cope with your unhealthy thoughts?

C Check your understanding. Go to page 61.

Step ② Tell your story

A THINK In your online course, you thought about a time when unhealthy thoughts affected you in a negative way. What happened, and what did you do? Listen to the example.

B PAIRS Discuss your story.

C SHARE Tell your story to the class.

Step ③ Take away

A PAIRS Use your notes from the online module. Complete the chart with your ideas.

1. What leads to unhealthy thinking?
✓ Obsessing about past errors
✓ ______
✓ ______

2. To avoid unhealthy thoughts ...	
DO	**DON'T**
✓ Consider all aspects of a situation	✓ ______
✓ ______	✓ ______
✓ ______	✓ ______
✓ ______	
✓ ______	
✓ ______	

B SHARE Compare your answers with the class. Can you add more ideas to the list?

Step 4 Activate your knowledge

A THINK Read the situations and the negative thoughts. Why are they unhealthy? How might you change each thought into a healthy one? Take notes.

SITUATION: Your teacher asked a question in class and you gave the wrong answer.

YOU THINK: "I'm so stupid! I should have known the answer to the question. Maybe I should switch to an easier class."

SITUATION: You called your friend last week, but she hasn't called you back.

YOU THINK: "I must have said something to offend her and now she's mad at me. That's why she's not calling me back!"

SITUATION: Your friend invited you to go camping. You've never gone camping before.

YOU THINK: "Camping seems pretty dangerous. There are a lot of wild animals in the woods. And we'll be far away from hospitals. What if something goes wrong? I'd better not go."

SITUATION: You got a flat tire on the way to work. You were late for a meeting with your manager.

YOU THINK: "These things always happen to me! Now I'm probably going to get fired! This is a disaster!"

SITUATION: You planned to exercise for an hour before work, but you overslept and now you don't have time.

YOU THINK: "If I don't have time to exercise for an hour, there's no point in exercising at all. I guess I'm not working out today."

B PAIRS Role-play a situation and its unhealthy thought. Give advice for improving negative thinking. Use these questions to guide your conversation, then repeat with a different situation.

1. Identify the thinking trap. What negative emotions are you feeling?

   ____

2. Is there a rational explanation for the situation?

   ____

3. How can you change the negative thought into a constructive one?

   ____

4. What can you do to avoid this thinking trap in the future?

   ____

C SHARE Present your advice to the class.

Step 5 Project

A PAIRS In your online course, you chose a technique to improve your thinking habits. Which one did you choose? Tell your partner about it. Read the example.

I kept a gratitude journal. It was actually really fun! I realized that I have so much to be grateful for. First, I wrote down big things like family, friends, and my home. But after a few days, I had to find something new, so I started writing smaller things like "a walk in the woods" and "my morning coffee." After ten days, I really started noticing how much better I felt. And little things that used to upset me weren't bothering me as much.

B SHARE Share your experience with the class.

Step 6 Talk!

PAIRS Read the quotes related to healthy thinking and then discuss the questions.

"The mind is everything. What you think you become."
– Buddha

"The positive thinker sees the invisible, feels the intangible, and achieves the impossible."
– Winston Churchill

"There are two ways to live: you can live as if nothing is a miracle; you can live as if everything is a miracle."
– Albert Einstein

"Keep your face to the sunshine and you cannot see the shadow."
– Helen Keller

- What do you think these quotes mean? Explain each one.
- Do you agree or disagree with these ideas about positive thinking? Explain.
- Which of the quotes do you relate to the most? Why?
- Do you know other quotes about being positive? Share.

Step 7 Going forward

A PAIRS In your online course, you reflected on how you would handle the situations in your life after studying more about healthy thinking. Discuss. Listen to the example.

B SHARE Present your ideas to the class.

VOCABULARY PRACTICE
Go to page 81.

I can describe ways to maintain healthy thinking. ☐

9 MODULE

Social Responsibility

Assessing Cultural Differences

DISCUSSION STRATEGIES

Go to page 68.

Step 1 Get started

A Refresh your memory! Watch the *What You'll Learn* video.

B Look at the photo. What kind of challenges might culturally diverse teams encounter? How can they solve them? What can they do to avoid future misunderstandings?

C Check your understanding. Go to page 62.

Step ② Tell your story

A THINK In your online course, you thought about a time when you were in a situation at work where cultural differences led to misunderstandings. What happened and how did you solve the issue? Listen to the example.

B PAIRS Discuss your story.

C SHARE Tell your story to the class.

Step ③ Take away

A PAIRS Review your notes from the online module. Then match the two parts of the sentence.

____ 1. People in cultures with a high-power distance score tend to

____ 2. In an individualist culture, people are more likely to value

____ 3. In so-called "feminine" cultures the focus is on

____ 4. In cultures with a lower uncertainty avoidance, people are

____ 5. Short-term oriented cultures are directed toward the

____ 6. Restrained cultures often have

a. their own well-being over the good of the group, their own opinions, their independence.

b. present and past performance.

c. value obedience, be more willing to accept their place in a workplace hierarchy.

d. more rules, fewer leisure activities, little or no idea of personal happiness as something to strive for.

e. more tolerant of atypical behavior, inclined to be more open-minded, more accepting of risk and ambiguity.

f. cooperation, sincerity, and maintaining relationships.

B SHARE Check your answers with the class.

Step ④ Activate your knowledge

A THINK Listen and read conversations. Discuss each situation using Hofstede's dimensions of culture. What is the conflict? Which dimension of culture is causing the conflict?

The Six Dimensions of Culture	
1. Power distance	4. Uncertainty avoidance
2. Individualism versus Collectivism	5. Long-term versus Short-term orientation
3. Masculinity versus Femininity	6. Indulgence versus Retraint

1. TERESA AND MATEO

Teresa works for Books 4 Kids, a nonprofit organization that focuses on developing reading and writing skills in young children. Mateo is in charge of a charitable foundation that provides money for the organization's work.

2. AMARA AND LUCAS

Amara and Lucas co-own a high-end clothing company that focuses on classic, wellmade clothes. They are discussing ways to expand the business.

3. WILL AND MINATO

Will is a research assistant at a university. He is meeting with his manager, Minato, for his annual performance review.

B PAIRS Discuss each conflict with a partner. How can the people use Hofstede's framework to manage the conflict? How might they benefit from their cultural differences?

C SHARE Present your idea to the class.

Step ⑤ Project

A PAIRS **In your online course, you rated yourself on your cultural dimensions and compared your score with your own country and another country. Tell your partner about it. Read the example.**

I'm from Japan. I scored myself 60 on power distance, 35 on individualism, 50 on masculinity, 90 on uncertainty avoidance, 80 on long-term orientation, and 30 on indulgence. I looked up the scores for Japan and most of them are pretty similar to my individual scores. But one thing I noticed that was interesting was that I scored a lot lower on masculinity. I was surprised to see the Japanese score for masculinity so high because I think Japanese people focus a lot on cooperation. I also looked up the United States, as a comparison. The scores were the exact opposite of mine in almost every category!

B SHARE **Discuss your analysis with the class.**

Step ⑥ Talk!

PAIRS **Look at the bar graph showing the United States' scores according to Hofstede's Cultural Dimensions. Then discuss the questions.**

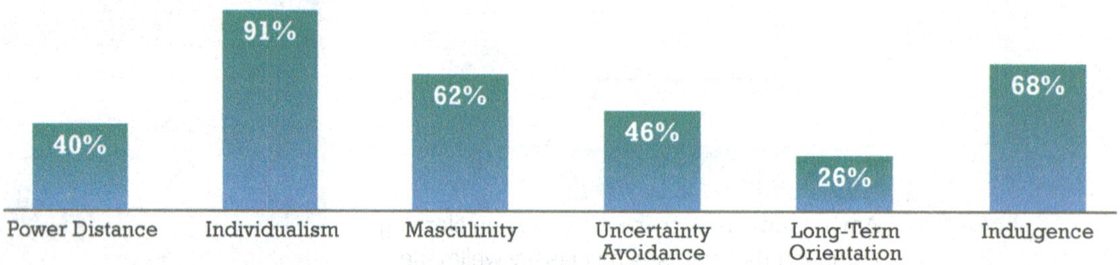

(Score range per dimension: 0–100)

- Are any of these scores surprising to you? Why?
- What kind of cultural misunderstandings would an American likely face in your country? Explain.
- What do the high score for individualism and the low score for long-term orientation suggest about how Americans are likely to behave at work?
- What do the above average scores for masculinity and indulgence suggest about what Americans value?

> Note: If you want to see the scores for your own or another country, go online and search for "Hofstede's Cultural Dimensions" and "Country."

Step ⑦ Going forward

A PAIRS **In your online course, you reflected on how you can use the information to work more smoothly with other people. Discuss. Listen to the example.**

B SHARE **Present your ideas to the class.**

VOCABULARY PRACTICE
Go to page 82.

I can explain Hofstede's cultural dimensions. ☐

10

MODULE

Branding

Personal Branding Mistakes

DISCUSSION STRATEGIES

Go to page 68.

Step 1 Get started

A Refresh your memory! Watch the *What You'll Learn* video.

B Look at the photo. The woman is shooting a video for her personal brand on social media. What should she do to avoid personal branding mistakes?

C Check your understanding. Go to page 63.

Step ② Tell your story

A THINK In your online course, you thought about a time you or someone you know made a mistake with a personal brand. What happened and how was the issue resolved? Listen to the example.

B PAIRS Discuss your story.

C SHARE Tell your story to the class.

Step ③ Take away

A PAIRS Review your notes from the online module on how to create a personal brand and handle brand mistakes. Complete the chart with the words in the box.

strengths blame weaknesses skills apologize opportunities
your message threats your public image desire personal story
professional and private who you really are

DO	DON'T
✔ SWOT analysis—Make a list of ______, ______, ______, ______	✔ Make false claims about your ______
✔ Consider your audience and what they ______	✔ Create a mismatch between ______ and ______
✔ Capitalize on your ______ ______	✔ Mix ______ ______ lives.
✔ Be consistent and clear about ______	✔ Make excuses or ______ others for your mistakes
✔ Admit your mistake and ______	

B SHARE Compare your ideas with the class. Can you add more to the list?

Step 4 Activate your knowledge

A THINK Think about your own brand. What are your goals and how can your brand help you achieve them? Read the survey questions and take notes.

1. What are your personal and professional goals?
2. Who is your target audience?
3. What are your core values?
4. What relevant experience do you have?
5. What skills or traits do you have that make you unique?
6. What skills can you improve?

B PAIRS Interview your partner. Discuss how you can use what you learned to develop and maintain your personal brand.

C PAIRS Read these branding mistakes. Why is each one a mistake? What are the possible consequences? How can you repair your brand and avoid making the same mistake in the future?

You have worked as a film critic for many years. Now you want to become a book critic, but all the content on your personal website is about movies.

You wrote a blog post expressing an unpopular opinion on a controversial political issue. The post went viral and offended a lot of your clients.

On your personal website, you say that you have several years of programming experience, but you've really only taken a few programming classes at university.

You recently attended an important conference in your industry. The CEO of your company was there, too. He overheard you complaining about your job and your company.

You own a local hardware store. The store has been in your family for three generations, and you have worked there since you were very young. This history is important to you, but you don't mention it in your marketing materials.

You own a successful restaurant chain. You opened the first restaurant because you wanted to focus on preparing healthy food. In interviews, you often talk about your successes growing your business, but you rarely talk about healthy food.

D SHARE Share your ideas with the class.

Step 5 Project

A PAIRS In your online course, you interviewed someone about their personal brand. Tell your partner about it. Read the example.

I interviewed a friend who has a really strong online presence. She is on several social media networks, and she also has a personal website. She told me that she tries to be consistent across all of these platforms. She feels like her core values are being adventurous and curious about other people, which make her both a great listener and a good innovator. Her travel experiences reflect those values, too. I couldn't really find any mistakes in her personal brand. I think she's done a great job of projecting an accurate image of herself and of representing her best qualities. category!

B SHARE Share your findings with the class.

Step 6 Talk!

PAIRS Read these common personal branding mistakes. How serious are they? Rank them from 1 (most serious) to 10 (least serious). Explain your reasons. Discuss.

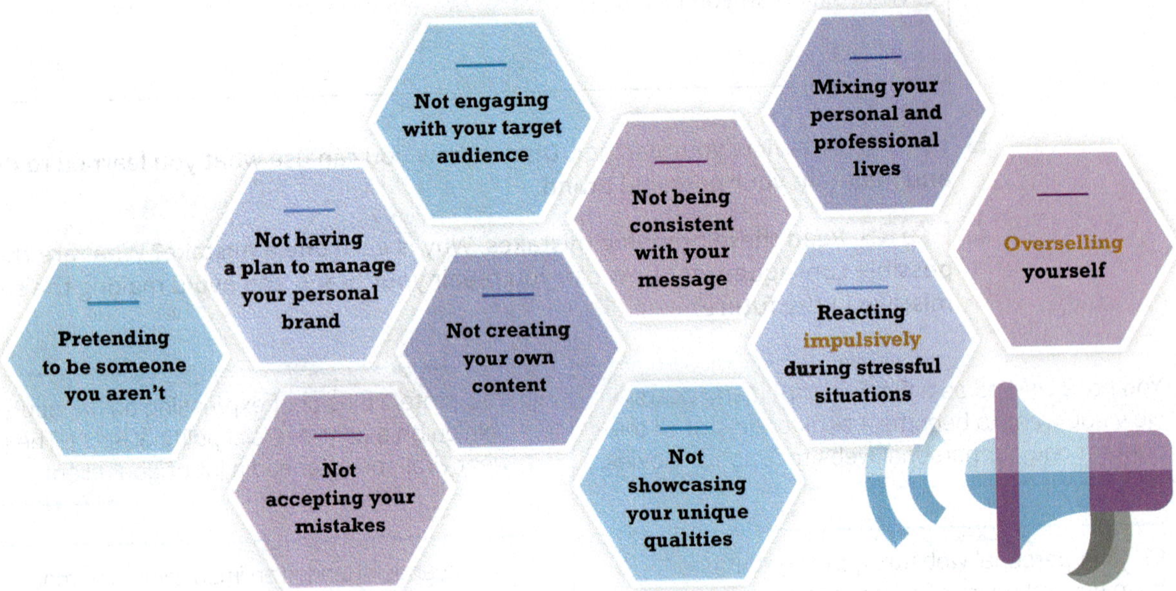

Step 7 Going forward

A PAIRS In your online course, you reflected on how you can avoid personal branding mistakes after studying more about it. Discuss. Listen to the example.

B SHARE Present your ideas to the class.

VOCABULARY PRACTICE
Go to page 83.

I can describe ways to avoid personal branding mistakes and strategies to fix mistakes if they occur. ☐

11

MODULE

Job Search

Building Your Career

DISCUSSION STRATEGIES

Go to page 68.

Step 1 Get started

A Refresh your memory! Watch the *What You'll Learn* video.

B Look at the photo. What would you suggest to people who want to build their careers? Have you taken any steps to build your career?

C Check your understanding. Go to page 64.

Step ② Tell your story

A THINK In your online course, you thought about a time when you were in a situation where you felt you needed to do something more to build your career. What did you do, and what happened? Listen to the example.

B PAIRS Discuss your story.

C SHARE Tell your story to the class.

Step ③ Take away

A PAIRS Review your notes from the online module. Match the phrases to answer the questions about building your career.

persuasion skills	expertise and knowledge
attending conferences, and events	to have more happiness and job satisfaction
to stand out to recruiters	getting professional development courses through e-learning platforms
active listening skills	teamwork skills
listening to podcasts, and watching videos	

1. Why is professional development important?

- *to have a successful professional life*
- ____________________
- ____________________

2. How can you develop skills?

- *attending in-company training*
- ____________________
- ____________________
- ____________________

3. What skills are needed to build your career?

a. Soft business skills, such as emotional intelligence, ____________________, ____________________, and ____________________.

b. Hard skills including ____________________ both in one's field and in one's tech abilities.

B SHARE Check your answers with the class. Can you think of other ways to build your career?

Step 4 Activate your knowledge

A PAIRS **Read and discuss each situation. Think of advice to help the people grow their careers. Use the questions to guide your discussion.**

1. Why is career growth important at this stage of each person's career?
2. How can they demonstrate career growth?
3. What areas should they focus on for professional development?
4. What can they do to pursue their professional development goals?

1 PURVI

has worked as an architect for several years. Over time, she has worked on larger and more complex projects. She enjoys her work, but she has recently become bored. She feels like she is ready for a new challenge. She wants to move up the corporate ladder to become a manager. Unfortunately, management positions at her company do not become available very often. She is trying to decide whether to pursue a promotion or look for a new job.

2 MINATO

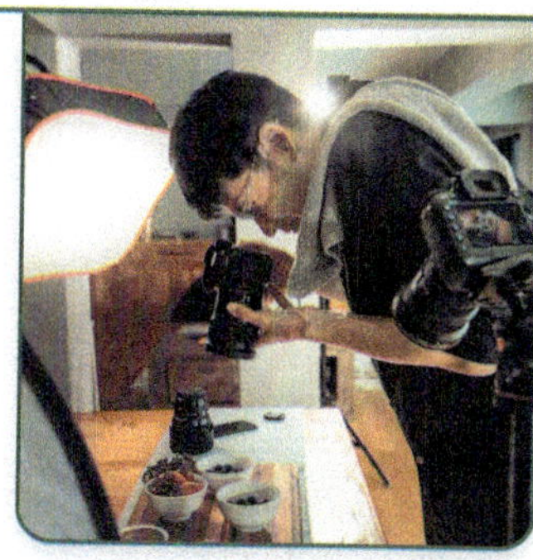

is a freelance photographer. He loves photography, but working as a freelancer can be frustrating. He is very busy not only with photography, but also with invoices and contracts. He does not have much time for networking. It is difficult to find clients because there is a lot of competition with other photographers. He is looking for ways to grow his career and become more competitive. He knows he needs to upskill, but he is not sure what skills to focus on.

3 BRIANNA

has been a psychologist for more than 15 years. She is very experienced and very skilled in her field. She loves working with people, especially with families. She wants to both develop her skills and share her expertise. She is looking for opportunities to grow in her profession, but she doesn't want to become a manager or administrator. She has thought about teaching psychology at a university, but she has never been a teacher and does not know how to make that transition.

4 JOE

has a lot of experience working in restaurants in different positions. He changes jobs every year or two. He has worked as a waiter, a cook, and a host. Most recently, he worked as an assistant manager at a popular restaurant that gets very busy on weekends. Now, he is interviewing for a job as a restaurant manager He is not sure how to explain all his job hopping.

B PAIRS **Discuss your own career growth. Why is developing your career important to you? What plans do you have for building your career? Do you have any advice for your partner?**

C SHARE **Present your ideas to the class.**

Step 5 Project

A PAIRS **In your online course, you identified skills to develop and steps you would take to develop them. Tell your partner about it. Read the example.**

The soft skills I think I have already are being able to listen really well and communicate clearly. I think I'm not as good at being persuasive, so that's a skill I'd like to develop. I'm going to pay attention when I'm in meetings and take notes about the strategies that other people use to be persuasive. For hard skills, I'm already good at most of the software that my company uses, but I'd like to become more familiar with how to use and leverage different social media platforms. I'm going to take some online tutorials to learn about the different possibilities on each platform. I'm also going to set up some private accounts just to practice using them.

B SHARE **Share your plan with the class.**

Step 6 Talk!

PAIRS **Read the statistics about career development and discuss the questions.**

74% of employees say that one of the biggest factors that prevents them from reaching their full potential is a lack of professional development opportunities.

Only 29% of companies provide a coherent learning and development plan for their staff.

Research shows that companies spending over $1,500 on their staff's learning and development have 24% higher annual profit.

59% of employees say they weren't given any workplace training; they learned most of their skills by themselves.

93% of employees say that a clear learning and development program would increase their engagement level.

94% of employees say they would continue working for the same company longer if they were provided with career development opportunities.

- Are any of these facts surprising to you? Why?
- Do you think that employees should take full advantage of development opportunities provided by their company? Why?
- What kind of learning and development opportunities would you hope for or expect from your employer? Why?

Step 7 Going forward

A PAIRS **In your online course, you reflected on how you can use the information in this module to build your career. Discuss. Listen to the example.**

B SHARE **Present your ideas to the class.**

VOCABULARY PRACTICE
Go to page 84.

I can explain ways to build my career. ☐

12

MODULE

Interviewing

Following up After an Interview

DISCUSSION STRATEGIES

Go to page 68.

Step ① Get started

A Refresh your memory! Watch the *What You'll Learn* video.

B Look at the photo. How should she follow up after the job interview?

C Check your understanding. Go to page 65.

Step ② Tell your story

A THINK In your online course, you thought about a time when you or someone you know followed up after a job interview. What did you do or not do, and what happened as a result? Listen to the example.

B PAIRS Discuss your story.

C SHARE Tell your story to the class.

Step ③ Take away

A PAIRS Review your notes from the online module and complete the sentences about following up after an interview.

Send a brief thank-you note by ____________ within ____________ hours of the interview.

Include the following four points in your thank-you note:

1. ____________.
2. ____________.
3. ____________.
4. ____________.

Proofread it before sending to avoid these mistakes, ____________.

Do not discuss your interview on ____________ and never try to contact ____________ on social media.

B SHARE Check your ideas with the class. Can you add more ideas?

Step 4 Activate your knowledge

A PAIRS Imagine that you've just interviewed for a job. It went well and you believe that you would be a good fit for the position. What should you do next? Make a list of 3–5 Do's and Don'ts that you learned from podcast.

Dos	Don'ts

B PAIRS Write a thank-you note to the interviewer (based on any job that interests you).

C PAIRS Proofread your note. Use this checklist.

Proofreading checklist:

- Uses an appropriate greeting
- Not too long or wordy
- Maintains a professional tone
- Free of typing mistakes
- Free of spelling and punctuation errors
- Uses an appropriate sign-off

D SHARE Exchange thank-you notes with another pair. Would you invite them for a second interview? Why or why not?

Step 5 Project

A PAIRS In your online course, you chose to interview a job recruiter, someone in a Human Resources department, or someone who got a job in the past few years. Tell your partner who you chose and what you learned. Read the example.

I asked a job recruiter in my LinkedIn network to answer the questions. He told me that he appreciates a candidate who writes a short, prompt thank-you note. He said that he doesn't look for new information in a thank-you note but just wants to see an expression of gratitude, as well as something that indicates the candidate's strong interest in the position. He said the most common mistake is when candidates write notes that are too casual, where they act like they are friends with the interviewer. He said this is really off-putting! Finally, he said he thinks it is fine for candidates to request feedback, even if he isn't always able to give it.

B SHARE Compare your notes with the class.

Step 6 Talk!

PAIRS Read some common mistakes that job seekers make when following-up after an interview. How serious are they? Rank them from 1 (most serious) to 9 (least serious). Explain your reasons.

- ☐ Sending a thank-you note minutes after the interview.
- ☐ Sending a follow-up email too soon.
- ☐ Sending multiple follow-up emails within a short timespan.
- ☐ Contacting a recruiter by phone after they've requested communication by email.
- ☐ Sending a very long follow-up email.
- ☐ Using the wrong name or job title of the person you're following up with writing with an inappropriate informal tone.
- ☐ Sending an email with errors in punctuation or spelling.
- ☐ Not including the interview date or job title in your email.
- ☐ Trying to connect with the recruiter on social media.

Step 7 Going forward

A PAIRS In your online course, you reflected on how you can follow up after a job interview after studying more about it. Discuss. Listen to the example.

B SHARE Present your ideas to the class.

VOCABULARY PRACTICE Go to page 85.

I can describe ways to follow up after a job interview. ☐

CHECK YOUR UNDERSTANDING

Check your understanding 1

REFRESH YOUR MEMORY!

Review the Online Course material in your Resources.

Choose the best answers. More than one answer may be correct in some items.

1 **Speaking professionally is important mainly because ____.**

- **a** it guarantees you'll succeed in your tasks
- **b** it makes you feel more important and powerful
- **c** it leads to better relationships at work

2 **Speaking professionally means ____.**

- **a** speaking with confidence and conviction and using the right tone
- **b** speaking hesitantly and quietly if you are not sure of what to say
- **c** sounding friendly and interested in other people

3 **What are some ways you can help yourself speak more confidently?**

- **a** Make a list of talking points before meetings.
- **b** Give yourself time in a conversation by saying *Let me think about that.*
- **c** Always answer people right away, even if you are not sure.

4 **How can you speak with conviction?**

- **a** Speak very loudly and with emotion.
- **b** Speak clearly, without mumbling.
- **c** Avoid using fillers like *uh* or *like*.

5 **Correct use of intonation can help you sound ____.**

- **a** professional and confident
- **b** uninterested and distant
- **c** friendly and interested

6 **Natasha manages a restaurant. One employee suggests that the restaurant needs to redesign the kitchen. But the restaurant is not doing well financially and cannot afford to do this. Natasha tries to use sarcasm as she responds. She laughs and says, "Well, sure. Right. That's a *great* idea. Maybe when we make an extra 10,000 dollars some night!" What is the problem with this response?**

- **a** The employee might think that Natasha will follow the suggestion.
- **b** It sounds like Natasha is not interested in the employee's suggestion.
- **c** It sounds like Natasha is insulting the employee and making fun of the suggestion.

7 **Teresa works for an international software developer. She is working on a report about recent sales trends in different regions of the world. Her manager stops her in the hall and asks her a question about sales in Southeast Asia. Teresa feels nervous and cannot remember the information off the top of her head. The best course of action would be to ____.**

- **a** make up the information and correct it later if she is wrong
- **b** say that she wants to check the figures and get back to him later
- **c** tell her manager that she doesn't know the answer

8 **Jun is a sales clerk in a department store. A customer comes in and asks him for his advice on buying a present for a teenager. Jun speaks softly and says: "Oh, well, um, you could get, like, a sweatshirt maybe. Or, I don't know, maybe there are some things in the electronics department." To sound more professional, Jun should have ____.**

- **a** spoken more softly and calmly
- **b** prepared notes for himself
- **c** avoided using fillers as he spoke

9 **Petra works in the design department for a website developer. At a meeting to discuss ideas for a new client's website, she presents her idea. Another person on the team says, "That sounds crazy. What on Earth makes you think the client would like something like that?" Petra probably feels ____.**

- **a** hurt, because the person used an aggressive tone
- **b** confident, because the person spoke clearly and strongly
- **c** confused, because the person spoke hesitantly

Check your understanding 2

REFRESH YOUR MEMORY!

Review the Online Course material in your Resources.

Choose the best answers. More than one answer may be correct in some items.

1 **Presentation skills are important because ____.**

- **a** they can help you succeed in your career
- **b** they are a necessity for many positions
- **c** they can help you organize your ideas

2 **When creating a presentation, what is one of the first things you should consider?**

- **a** the design and layout of the slides
- **b** where to find good resources for research
- **c** the audience you will be speaking to

3 **When you plan a presentation, it is important to consider ____.**

- **a** whether and how you will involve the audience
- **b** what the purpose of the slides will be
- **c** how much data you can fit onto each slide

4 **What should you remember when designing slides?**

- **a** With smaller fonts, you can fit more information.
- **b** The images you use are less important than the bullet points.
- **c** The text on the slides should be concise and clear.

5 **When you give your presentation, remember to ____.**

- **a** read the bullet points from your slides
- **b** keep the audience engaged
- **c** move quickly from one topic to the next

6 **What is the purpose of using phrases like *for example* and *finally* during a presentation?**

- **a** It gives you time to pause and think while you are speaking.
- **b** It helps to engage your audience and maintain their interest.
- **c** It helps the audience follow your thoughts and understand connections.

7 **Tal gave a presentation to his company giving some ideas on how to think more creatively. He had a lot of points to cover and not very much time, so he spoke quickly throughout the whole presentation. At the end, there were a lot of questions and the presentation ended up running late. Next time, Tal could ____.**

- **a** reduce the number of points and speak more slowly with pauses
- **b** add images to his slides so that he wouldn't have to say as much
- **c** change the pitch of his voice so that people understand the key points more

8 **Diana works in sales at a large company. Her manager asked her to present the company's upcoming goals at their monthly meeting. Diana prepared slides with clear charts and images. When she gave the presentation, she stood in one place and looked at the slides to help her remember what to say. At the end, she turned around and asked the audience if they had questions. They had no questions and she thought they looked bored. Diana should have ____.**

- **a** crossed the room frequently to address people on both sides
- **b** made eye contact with the audience while she was speaking
- **c** used more charts and images in her slides

9 **Elsa just started working for an advertising company. She had to give a presentation to a client. She planned the presentation well and designed clear slides. But when she had to give the presentation, she forgot a lot of her talking points. The client was disappointed and decided not to work with her company. Next time, Elsa should ____.**

- **a** create bullet points that she can read word for word
- **b** write exactly what she'll say and read from the paper
- **c** rehearse more ahead of time and take notes

10 **Kai works for a furniture design company. He recently had to present some new product ideas at the company meeting. He used purple font on a black background and he included a lot of images of the products. He kept his bullet points simple and not too wordy, and he used an Arial font in 24 point size. Did Kai design his slides well?**

- **a** Yes. He did everything correctly in designing his slides.
- **b** No. He should have used fewer images and more bullet points.
- **c** No. He should have used a white or light background and black font.

Check your understanding 3

REFRESH YOUR MEMORY!
Review the Online Course material in your Resources.

Choose the best answers. More than one answer may be correct in some items.

1 **Cascading goals can best be described as ____.**
- **a** a way of planning a company's short-term strategies
- **b** a way of creating good teamwork in different departments
- **c** a way of communicating goals across all levels of the organization

2 **When a company has cascading goals, every level of the company has goals that ____.**
- **a** are directly related to the company's overall business strategy
- **b** are specifically written for them by the top level of management
- **c** allow them to determine their own priorities

3 **What are the benefits of cascading goals?**
- **a** They allow workers some creativity in coming up with their own objectives.
- **b** They provide clarity and direction and allow people to feel like they are contributing.
- **c** They help teams communicate more clearly with each other.

4 **What are some reasons cascading goals might fail?**
- **a** The company has not communicated the goals clearly.
- **b** The process goes too quickly before everyone has a chance to give input.
- **c** The company is large and it takes too long for the goals to reach all departments.

5 **In order to create success with cascading goals, it is important to ____.**
- **a** communicate clear goals written in the SMART format
- **b** have regular meetings to discuss progress and reward achievements
- **c** give workers complete independence as they work toward their goals

6 **A company that designs small home appliances wants to increase its profits by 20% over the next year. To help ensure that they reach this goal, the company leadership can ____.**
- **a** email the entire company to tell them the goal
- **b** invite employees to offer suggestions for achieving the goal
- **c** meet with department heads to create plans for communicating and implementing the goal at each level

7 **Fernando supervises administrative staff at a hospital. One of the hospital's goals this year is to improve communication among medical teams. Fernando used this information to create smaller goals. He then wrote these goals down and sent the list to his team. In what ways did Fernando successfully use the concept of cascading goals?**
- **a** He broke down the larger goal into smaller, related goals.
- **b** He clearly communicated how individual goals aligned to the larger hospital goal.
- **c** He motivated his workers by making them feel part of a shared vision.

8 **The leadership of a large company introduced their new 10-year vision at a recent company-wide meeting. To make sure that employees know specifically how to contribute toward these goals, the leadership can ____.**
- **a** send out an email reminding people of the new company goals
- **b** train department heads in setting aligned goals for their departments
- **c** set specific SMART goals for each person in the company

9 **Peter is the CEO of a chain of restaurants. He wants to expand the restaurant's vegetarian selections to appeal to a broader population and increase profits. To make sure he can reach this goal, Peter decides to cascade the goals to the wider organization. First, he should ____.**
- **a** meet with the franchise managers as a group to discuss the goal and how to implement it within their business locations
- **b** tell the franchise managers to start advertising that they are a vegetarian-friendly restaurant
- **c** email the chefs and tell them to come up with some new menu ideas

10 **Felix manages a team of software developers at a large company. He has worked with his team to create a set of goals that align with the company's overall goal. However, he has noticed that some of the employees don't seem to be making much progress toward their goals. Felix can improve this situation by ____.**
- **a** sending out an email with another overview of the company goals
- **b** asking workers to put in extra time to make sure they can make progress
- **c** scheduling regular meetings to make sure employees have what they need and know how to achieve their goals

Check your understanding 4

REFRESH YOUR MEMORY!

Review the Online Course material in your Resources.

Choose the best answers. More than one answer may be correct in some items.

1 Team spirit at work can be described as ____.

- **a** a management system that helps individuals work productively
- **b** the shared trust between co-workers that helps motivate them
- **c** a set of guidelines for people working together on a project

2 When working remotely, people ____.

- **a** feel more of a shared challenge
- **b** lose the possibility of instant feedback
- **c** usually don't work as hard

3 Regular, purposeful meetings help people ____.

- **a** feel like part of the group
- **b** have a calm, quiet working environment
- **c** understand their roles and tasks

4 If you have to hold a video conference, make sure that ____.

- **a** people turn off their cameras for privacy
- **b** people have the agenda in advance
- **c** someone takes notes and sends them out after

5 To help maintain team spirit when working remotely, ____.

- **a** schedule some "video hangouts" where people can socialize
- **b** spontaneously set team-building activities during status meetings
- **c** offer praise and encouragement often to teammates and employees

6 Stas is a manager of the design team at a home appliance company. His team recently transitioned to a hybrid schedule, with each person coming in once or twice a week. They hold online weekly status meetings, but Stas has noticed that these meetings are mostly short and task-focused. He thinks that the team has become less creative in coming up with new design ideas and improvements. He feels they worked better when everyone could share ideas throughout the day. The best way to improve the situation would be to ____.

- **a** send out an agenda before the status meetings, adding time for new proposals
- **b** try to find one day when all workers could be in the office together
- **c** give employees a mandatory team-building activity

7 Lana has just started a new remote job as a marketing assistant. The team keeps her very busy with research assignments and other tasks. She likes the work, but she doesn't get to interact very much with the team. She is sometimes not sure if they are happy with the work she is doing. She also feels the other team members know each other very well, and she doesn't feel like she is part of the group. To help her situation, Lana could ask ____.

- **a** to set up videoconferences with different team members to get feedback "in-person" on the work she is doing
- **b** the team to send her a clear list of her tasks each week
- **c** the team to set up some informal coffee hours online to get to know each other

8 Fernando manages the accounting department at his company. The office is currently fully remote. Fernando decided to set up regular status meetings via videoconference for his team. During these meetings, he always starts by recognizing some specific things people have accomplished since the last meeting. These meetings are valuable because they help people ____.

- **a** focus on the important tasks
- **b** feel motivated
- **c** see the bigger picture of what others are working on

9 Julia teaches engineering classes at a public college. Most of the classes are now online, and Julia thinks that her students seem less motivated. To help her students, Julia could ____.

- **a** set up more frequent classes and team assignments
- **b** set up some informal, online team competitions
- **c** set aside a little time in each class for socializing

10 Shuchang manages the sales team at his company. The team has started working mostly remotely, with a few workers coming into the office once or twice a week. Lately, Shuchang has noticed that morale seems low, and the employees don't seem to be working together as a team. Working remotely can affect how people feel in the workplace. What might be happening to Shuchang's team?

- **a** People feel they can get more things done without the team.
- **b** People feel isolated and less motivated.
- **c** People have lost the feeling of camaraderie and trust.

Check your understanding 5

REFRESH YOUR MEMORY!

Review the Online Course material in your Resources.

Choose the best answers. More than one answer may be correct in some items.

1 What is design thinking?

a an analytical method which helps people figure out issues with products

b a people-centered approach for creating innovative solutions to complex problems

c a tool companies use to help their employees better solve design problems independently

2 Design thinking requires ____.

a a collaborative effort

b a multidisciplinary team

c a common-sense attitude

3 Design thinking can help you ____.

a gain detailed information about what customers want

b brainstorm solutions to clear, simple problems

c come up with innovative ideas for complex problems

4 The order of the five steps for design thinking is ____.

a ideate, define, prototype, empathize, test

b define, prototype, ideate, test, empathize

c empathize, define, ideate, prototype, test

5 When brainstorming, it is important to ____.

a come up with a lot of ideas

b judge ideas quickly to eliminate unworkable ones

c stay focused on the target problem

6 The People's Bank wants to overhaul its mobile banking app in response to customer complaints about lack of user-friendliness. What would be the best first step for the bank to take, using a design thinking approach?

a Ask the technology design team to come up with ideas of what they can easily improve.

b Ask a group of customers to do in-depth interviews about their experiences with the app.

c Look at competitive products and create features similar to theirs.

7 Gordon's is a large department store with both physical stores and an online presence. Lately their sales have been falling, as customers turn to online warehouses that can sell goods more cheaply. Gordon's wants to come up with some new ideas and customer offerings in order to stay competitive. They will use a design approach in determining the best strategies. Which of the following problem statements best describes their issue and goal?

a In order to stay competitive in an increasingly online market, we need to come up with fresh, exciting customer incentives to shop with us.

b We're going to go out of business unless we come up with something that online stores can't offer.

c So that we can keep our customers happy, we should offer a greater variety of products at deeper discounts.

8 Carlos works for a company that makes small home appliances. He was in a brainstorming session to come up with new ideas for products based on customer needs. Carlos had an idea for a new product, but it was a very unusual idea, so he decided not to say anything. At the end of the session, the team had a small list of possible products, but none of them were very different or new. Next time the team should ____.

a invite a larger group of people to join the brainstorming session

b stay more focused on what the customer needs were

c make it clear that even unusual ideas would be welcomed

9 WellWorld is a company that makes a variety of wellness-related apps. They recently conducted a round of customer surveys, and based on the results they want to develop a new app. They held a brainstorming session and came up with a long list of possible ideas. Their next step is ____.

a assigning teams to develop prototypes for each of the ideas

b using "convergent thinking" to narrow down the list to the best ideas

c getting in-house testers to figure out which ideas are the most workable

10 TechPro, a company that makes computer parts, has developed the prototype for a new mouse that can relieve pain in the user's wrists. They have completed in-house testing and learned of some problems in the mouse design. Their next step is ____.

a refining the prototype and do some more in-house testing

b planning larger-scale testing with target customer groups

c designing a brand-new prototype using a different design plan

Check your understanding 6

REFRESH YOUR MEMORY!
Review the Online Course material in your Resources.

Choose the best answers. More than one answer may be correct in some items.

1 **Change leadership can best be defined as a way to ____.**
- **a** bring about large changes that benefit a company
- **b** head-hunt the best new senior management
- **c** ask employees to change their working methods or schedules

2 **One of the most important qualities of good change leaders is that they can ____.**
- **a** implement change alone and without unnecessary communication
- **b** make decisions quickly about how to downsize effectively
- **c** communicate a vision clearly and keep employees motivated

3 **It is important to communicate clearly when downsizing so that employees ____.**
- **a** know who is leaving the company and when
- **b** feel respected and have some clarity on the situation
- **c** can make their own decisions about whether to leave

4 **An enthusiastic change leader can ____.**
- **a** make sure the organization doesn't give up important projects
- **b** keep employees satisfied with their current skill sets
- **c** motivate employees and help them think creatively

5 **Change leaders have to ____.**
- **a** be committed to the change and willing to give it time
- **b** lay off any employees who disagree with the change
- **c** develop a clear and practical strategy

6 **Change leaders can maintain morale by ____.**
- **a** making sure not to talk about challenges that employees may have
- **b** sharing the vision for keeping the company innovative
- **c** letting employees figure out their own ways of dealing with the change

7 **Gina is on the management team of a company that is planning to downsize soon as they streamline their operations. The employees are all anxious, and many of them seem very unmotivated at work. To help this situation, Gina can ____.**
- **a** offer support and keep the lines of communication open
- **b** tell employees that the harder they work, the more likely they won't get laid off
- **c** send out the list of people who will be laid off as soon as she has it

8 **Theo manages the IT department of a large company. The company is planning to overhaul its technological systems and software. Theo's team is unfamiliar with most of the new programs, since they are very new. When he discusses the changes with his manager, he should ____.**
- **a** recommend that they continue using the old software, since people know it better
- **b** ask his manager to let him hire all new employees with more up-to-date skills
- **c** explain that his team will need training sessions to get them up to speed

9 **Mei works with a company which helps high school students apply for college. The company is planning to expand and offer consulting for younger children as well. Mei has been told by her manager to explain the change to her team. She knows that some of them may be uncomfortable, but she wants to get the team excited about the change. She calls a meeting and says, "This is a great opportunity for the company to grow, and for all of us to expand our skills. We'll be offering some development sessions for anyone interested in working with the younger groups, and I invite your suggestions as to how the company can support all of you through this change." What change leadership strategies is Mei using?**
- **a** explaining the benefits of the change
- **b** offering support and training to employees
- **c** developing a clear strategy for the company

10 **Carlos owns a chain of hair salons. Lately, the company has been losing business to more modern salons. Carlos calls a meeting with his salon managers to get their ideas on why they are losing business. He asks them for their suggestions on what changes the company might make in order to stay competitive and explains his idea of introducing skin care treatments and massage rooms to attract customers. What change leadership strategy is Carlos using?**
- **a** sharing his vision for how to keep the company competitive
- **b** inviting employee participation in the process of change
- **c** explaining the advantages of making changes to the managers and their staff

Check your understanding 7

REFRESH YOUR MEMORY!
Review the Online Course material in your Resources.

Choose the best answers. More than one answer may be correct in some items.

1 **If you have a growth mindset, you are likely to ____.**

a take on challenges only if you are certain you can succeed
b understand that mistakes are something you can learn from
c believe that your intelligence and abilities are fixed

2 **A growth mindset can give you the ability to ____.**

a persist
b avoid difficulties
c learn new things

3 **Which of these examples shows someone who has a growth mindset?**

a a student who decides to drop a course because it is difficult, and her grades are not good
b a scientist who tries out new theories because he hasn't yet succeeded with an experiment
c a business person who asks not to speak at conferences because he knows he isn't good at it

4 **To develop a growth mindset, you should ____.**

a keep trying a strategy several times
b ignore the mistakes that you make
c question why you made a mistake

5 **Jing is taking a biology course at a university. She is finding the assigned readings very difficult, and she is starting to think that she is not smart enough for this course. She can approach this problem with a growth mindset by ____.**

a asking the professor for strategies to understand the readings
b looking into tutoring possibilities to support her in the readings
c looking into what other courses might be better for her

6 **Marc works for the accounting department of a company that sells furniture. The company has decided to upgrade the software it uses for financing. Marc is unfamiliar with the new software, and he has been making a lot of mistakes with it. He can approach this problem with a growth mindset by ____.**

a asking the company to consider switching back to the old software
b telling his manager that he needs some extra training on the new program
c looking for work at another company that uses the software he knows well

7 **Dal has played the violin since he was young. He auditioned to play with his college orchestra, but he did not make it. He feels embarrassed and does not know what to do. He enjoys the violin but thinks he is not good enough to continue. He can approach this problem with a growth mindset by ____.**

a deciding to stop playing violin and focus more on his college studies
b practicing a lot by himself and with a teacher and audition again
c complaining to the orchestra director that the audition was not judged fairly

8 **Tania is a salesperson at a department store. Recently she was promoted to sales manager. One of her responsibilities is to write reviews for the workers she manages. When she submitted her first set of reviews, her supervisor asked her to re-do them because they were not in the correct format. Tania feels embarrassed and is afraid she'll make mistakes again. She can approach this problem with a growth mindset by ____.**

a reminding herself that it was her first time, and she can learn from the errors
b asking her supervisor to give her an example of the correct format
c asking the workers she manages to write their own self-assessment next time

Check your understanding 8

REFRESH YOUR MEMORY!
Review the Online Course material in your Resources.

Choose the best answers. More than one answer may be correct in some items.

1 Healthy thinking gives people a way to ____.
- a improve their physical fitness
- b get past negative feelings
- c succeed in all their tasks

2 If I think, "I'm always anxious when I speak in front of people. I must be terrible at it," what kind of negative self-talk is this an example of?
- a blaming yourself for mistakes you have made
- b making assumptions about what other people think
- c irrationally thinking that feelings reflect reality

3 The first step you need to take in order to improve negative thinking is ____.
- a recognizing when you are engaging in negative thinking
- b stopping your negative thoughts by going on a walk
- c talking to a friend to ask if your thoughts are rational

4 To develop healthy thinking, you can ____.
- a practice appreciating the things that are good in your life
- b try to forget about everything that happened in the past
- c imagine being successful and how that will feel

5 To overcome negative thinking, you can also try ____.
- a staying up late to think about things
- b eating a balanced diet
- c doing something active every day

6 Omar has to write a report at work. It is due this afternoon, but because of a technical problem on his computer, he lost all of his work. He thinks to himself, "Why does this always happen to me?" What thinking trap is Omar falling into?
- a jumping to conclusions
- b feeling like a victim
- c being too hard on himself

7 Chan-mi wrote an email this morning to the team she is collaborating with on a project. She asked people to respond with their thoughts on an idea she had. It is two hours later, and no one has responded. Chan-mi thinks, "They must think my idea was terrible." What thinking trap is Chan-mi falling into?
- a feeling like a victim
- b blaming herself for a mistake
- c jumping to conclusions

8 Manuel had a lot of things to do at work on Wednesday. He finished preparing a report, set up some necessary meetings, and contacted two clients to respond to questions that they had. He was supposed to contact a third client, but he ran out of time. He thought, "I should have scheduled my time better. I really could have called that client today. Now everything will be delayed and it will be my fault." What can Manuel say to himself to change his negative thoughts?
- a "Next time I really need to plan better."
- b "I'd better figure out how to apologize to the client."
- c "I accomplished a lot today. I'll call the client first thing tomorrow."

9 Kobi has been asked to give a presentation on a new hair coloring technique at the salon where he works. He is feeling very anxious about it. He thinks, "I've never done this before. What if I'm awful? No one will respect me." What can Kobi say to himself to change his negative thoughts?
- a "Everyone in the salon will understand. I just need to practice and do my best."
- b "It's not that important. It doesn't really matter if I mess up. I'll still use the new technique."
- c "The manager of the salon shouldn't ask stylists to do these kinds of presentations. It's so embarrassing."

10 Petra has to write a paper for her university class. She has written several papers for other classes, but she always hates it. She thinks she is a bad writer and that she won't be able to write a good paper for this class. To improve her thinking, Petra can ____.
- a ask her teacher if she can do something else instead of writing the paper
- b remember how she was able to write good essays in the past
- c remind herself that when she works hard at something, she is often successful

Check your understanding 9

REFRESH YOUR MEMORY!

Review the Online Course material in your Resources.

Choose the best answers. More than one answer may be correct in some items.

1 **In his theory of cultural dimensions, Hofstede provides ____.**

- **a** a way of measuring and understanding different cultural attitudes
- **b** six areas of concern for people who have different backgrounds
- **c** general descriptors for explaining the behavior of different people

2 **Cultures with a high score in collectivism usually ____.**

- **a** like to work together as part of a team
- **b** value ambitious personal goals
- **c** are focused on the larger organization they belong to

3 **Cultures with a long-term orientation are more likely to ____.**

- **a** try to achieve quick results
- **b** value persistence in working toward solutions
- **c** measure business success by comparing with the previous year

4 **"Indulgent" cultures place a high value on ____.**

- **a** happiness
- **b** restraint
- **c** rules

5 **In order to overcome misunderstandings that arise from cultural diversity, it is important to ____.**

- **a** consider how well other people meet your expectations
- **b** listen to other people's ideas with an open mind
- **c** have an awareness of one's own cultural perspective

6 **Claudia is at a foreign university. She is used to asking a lot of questions in her classes at home, but here the other students just listen and take notes. She is not sure what to do when she does not understand something. What cultural dimension does Claudia demonstrate?**

a high power distance **b** collectivism **c** femininity

7 **Liz has gone to work as a salesperson for an overseas branch of her company. She has noticed that the other salespeople there are highly competitive with each other. Liz is used to collaborating closely with her colleagues and developing strong relationships. What cultural dimension does Liz demonstrate?**

a high power distance **b** individualism **c** femininity

8 **Lucy has just started working for a new company. She has a lot of ideas about ways the company can bring in new clients. When she suggests the ideas, her manager listens but tells her that the company isn't interested in changing the way they do business. What cultural dimension does Lucy demonstrate?**

a low power distance **b** femininity **c** low uncertainty avoidance

9 **Pete has been hired as a manager in another country. He comes from a culture with a low power distance score, and is used to a collaborative approach where everyone gives suggestions during meetings. In a meeting with his new team, he asks for ideas, but no one responds. They respect Pete, but are used to being told what to do. Pete thinks they are quiet because they are unhappy with his management. How can Pete take steps to overcome this misunderstanding?**

- **a** He should consider the problem from a cultural perspective, and be aware that he might be misinterpreting his employees' behavior.
- **b** He could consider a different approach, such as inviting employees to submit written suggestions whenever they feel comfortable.
- **c** He can tell the employees that they will not succeed if they don't come up with ideas.

10 **Kathleen has started working for a company overseas, managing a team that develops new products. Kathleen comes from a culture where the focus is on group success rather than on individual achievements. At a meeting, Kathleen praised the team for coming up with a new product design. However, some of the team members felt offended that she did not mention them individually for their efforts and achievements. To address these different cultural expectations, Kathleen can ____.**

- **a** tell them that their collaborative effort is more important than their individual efforts
- **b** realize that her team may have a different perspective and accept it
- **c** praise the group for their collective efforts and also call out individuals' contributions

Check your understanding 10

REFRESH YOUR MEMORY!

Review the Online Course material in your Resources.

Choose the best answers. More than one answer may be correct in some items.

1 A personal brand is a way of ____.
- **a** showcasing what sets you apart from others
- **b** using social networks to compete for jobs
- **c** presenting your personal life to employers

2 Why is having a personal brand important?
- **a** It shows people the kinds of things you do outside of work.
- **b** It helps you stand out and be noticed by employers or managers.
- **c** It lets people know that you are comfortable with online branding.

3 Doing a SWOT analysis can help you by ____.
- **a** showing employers what you are good at
- **b** helping you identify strengths and areas for improvement
- **c** helping you use your professional web page in a targeted way

4 A common mistake with personal branding is ____.
- **a** not asking yourself questions about your core values
- **b** not mixing your personal life with your professional life
- **c** showing inconsistencies between your public image and how you really are

5 If you make a mistake with your brand, you should ____.
- **a** acknowledge it and apologize
- **b** listen to other people's feedback
- **c** try to figure out who was to blame

6 Thomas has just finished culinary school and he dreams of opening his own restaurant in New York City. Which of the following is an opportunity that he should outline as part of his SWOT analysis?
- **a** Most new restaurants in New York go out of business within five years.
- **b** Thomas's favorite teacher used to live in New York and has several contacts there.
- **c** Thomas has very good communication and organization skills.

7 Yuri is an accountant who has a goal of being a personal financial advisor. He is very good at understanding the human emotions behind decisions about money, and he has had many years of experience. He created a website to advertise his services. The website is very simple, listing his work experience and contact information. He knows the type of person he wants to attract, so he has listed the kinds of services that he knows they would need. But so far, he hasn't attracted new clients online. Yuri might be able to attract more clients online by ____.
- **a** highlighting his unique selling points in his website better
- **b** trying to be more persuasive when he speaks in person with potential clients
- **c** considering his target audience and what they are looking for

8 Winnie is a skin care consultant who works with all-natural products. Her brand is known for being trustworthy. She has set up her own web page to promote her services and the products she uses. Recently, she learned that one of the products on her website was not all-natural, as it had claimed. It is one of her favorite products, and one which she often recommends to clients. What should Winnie do?
- **a** Nothing. If it is a good product, she should just keep promoting it.
- **b** She should let her clients know about the product's false advertising.
- **c** She should stop advertising that product and find a suitable, all-natural alternative.

Check your understanding 11

REFRESH YOUR MEMORY!

Review the Online Course material in your Resources.

Choose the best answers. More than one answer may be correct in some items.

1 By developing your career, you can ____.
- **a** develop more work contacts
- **b** attain job satisfaction
- **c** look good to hiring managers

2 Why is it important for employees to learn new skills?
- **a** It keeps them relevant in their industry.
- **b** It makes their company a better place to work.
- **c** It helps them get promoted.

3 To help develop yourself professionally, you can ____.
- **a** complete at-work training programs
- **b** sign up for volunteer work in another field
- **c** engage in self-learning opportunities

4 Some examples of soft skills that can be developed are ____.
- **a** computer skills
- **b** language skills
- **c** persuasion skills

5 If your workplace does not offer training, ____.
- **a** your boss will sponsor you to take a course
- **b** you may find trainings online
- **c** you can try to take on new projects that help you develop

6 Hiro recently graduated from university and is now working as a graphic designer for a website developer. Hiro mainly works by himself, and he enjoys this. At his first performance review, his manager says his design work is great, but he suggests that Hiro should work on at least one team project. Why do you think the manager suggests this?
- **a** Teamwork skills are important for building a career.
- **b** Hiro can learn design skills from his co-workers.
- **c** Hiro is ready to be promoted to a management position.

7 Sonia has been working as an electrician for a few years. She is happy in her work but does not feel she is learning or gaining skills anymore. Sonia should ____.
- **a** think about changing her career
- **b** talk to her manager about ways to learn new skills
- **c** set up a training program at her company

8 Max has been working as a legal assistant for several years. He is interested in developing his career, so he talks to his boss about attending an upcoming convention. She tells him that she cannot let him attend now because the office is too busy. Max should ____.
- **a** call in sick and go to the convention anyway
- **b** find out if any of the presentations will be recorded so that he can watch later
- **c** ask his boss to discuss other potential growth opportunities

9 Mimi is a childcare worker. She enjoys what she does because she gets to work directly with children. She does not want to work in the kind of position where she has to perform more administrative tasks. What skills might be helpful to her anyway?
- **a** learning to work well on a team
- **b** getting some leadership experience
- **c** getting promoted to a managerial position

Check your understanding 12

REFRESH YOUR MEMORY!

Review the Online Course material in your Resources.

Choose the best answers. More than one answer may be correct in some items.

1 **After an interview, it is common courtesy to ____.**
- **a** leave the job interviewer alone
- **b** send a thank you note within 24 hours
- **c** call the interviewer the next day

2 **The best way to write a thank you note is to ____.**
- **a** hand write a card for a personal touch
- **b** send a long and detailed email to impress the interviewer
- **c** send a short email that covers a few main points

3 **A good thank you note will ____.**
- **a** show your gratitude for the opportunity
- **b** indicate your strong interest in the job
- **c** follow up on several interview questions

4 **When you don't hear back from the interviewer, ____.**
- **a** you should assume you have not gotten the job
- **b** it is helpful to call the interviewer regularly
- **c** send a short follow-up email after a week or two

5 **Thalia interviewed for a position as a nurse assistant. Now she wants to write a thank you note. In the note, she should make sure to say that she ____.**
- **a** enjoyed the interview
- **b** learned something about the interviewer
- **c** expects them to respond to her soon

6 **Gerard just interviewed to be an assistant restaurant manager. He thought the interview went really well. He got along very well with the manager who interviewed him. He is walking home now and considering how he should follow up. He should ____.**
- **a** text the manager while he is walking home and express his excitement
- **b** wait for a couple of hours, consider what to say, then write an email
- **c** wait for a couple of days, consider what to say, then call the manager

7 **Akiko interviewed for a position as a computer programmer. The interview went well, and now she is working on a thank you note. If she writes a successful thank you note, it will show that she ____.**
- **a** is grateful and interested
- **b** expects she will get the job
- **c** has good communication skills

8 **Fernando interviewed for a position in the Human Resources department of a large company. There were several other candidates for the position. Even though the interview went well, Fernando did not get the job. He should ____.**
- **a** post about the interview on his social media page
- **b** call the interviewer to ask for an explanation
- **c** move on and keep applying to other jobs

9 **Do-yun interviewed for a customer service position at a large media company. He thought the interviewer was really friendly and the interview went well. After writing a thank you note and waiting three weeks for a call back, he finally received the call: he didn't get the job. He wonders what he should have done to make a better impression. He could have ____.**
- **a** proofread his note and corrected the mistakes he made in spelling before sending it
- **b** written a follow-up email after a few weeks saying he was still interested in the position
- **c** called the interviewer after their meeting to say he enjoyed the interview and ask for feedback

DISCUSSION STRATEGIES

Discussion strategies

When you are in class or at work, you may need to take part in discussions. To successfully participate, you can use a number of different kinds of strategies. They include strategies that help you:

1 Work with others
2 Clarify what you hear or clarify what you say
3 Get and stay involved in the discussion
4 Organize your ideas

During each discussion in class, choose one kind of strategy you want to improve or one you think will be useful. Pick a phrase and try to use it during the in-class activities. Remember to always say the phrase in a polite way.

You can listen to the phrases and examples.

1 Working with others

Some strategies can make it easier to work with other people who are part of the discussion. If you can, try starting the discussion or helping to keep the discussion moving in the right direction. These strategies can help.

Management strategies	Sample phrases
a Starting the discussion	Is everyone ready? Let's get going. Who wants to kick things off?
b Asking others to participate	Who wants to offer their idea first? Does anyone have anything more to add? Who wants to chime in?
c Helping specific people to get involved	Lina, what do you think? Do you have any thoughts to add, Mikhail? Gina, any thoughts to share?
d Jumping in with talkative people	That's a good point. Now let's hear from everyone else. Thanks for that. And what does everyone else think? Great idea, Ilya! Now, let's ask everyone else their thoughts.
e Staying on the topic	That's interesting, but maybe I'm missing something. I don't see how that's really relevant to the topic. Let's discuss this at a later date. For now, we need to stay on task. I'm really sorry, but I don't see how that's related.
f Keeping the discussion moving	OK. So now let's move on to the next point. That's a good idea and we should talk about that next time. I'm afraid that we're going to run out of time if we don't move forward.
g Telling someone you can't hear them*	I'm sorry. I didn't hear what you said. Can you speak a little louder so everyone can hear you. Sorry! What was that?
h Telling someone they speak too fast*	I'm sorry. Can you say that a little slower? Can you talk slower, please? Sorry. I didn't catch what you said.

*You can also use clarification strategies to make sure you understood someone who is quiet or talks too quickly.

Discussion strategies

2 Clarifying

Sometimes, it is hard for you to understand what someone is saying or for others to understand you. Clarifying is a natural part of discussions. Even native speakers use these strategies because not everyone understands everything all the time!

Clarification strategies	Sample phrases	Examples
a Clarifying (when you didn't understand someone else)	▶ Sorry, but I don't understand. ▶ I'm not sure what you mean by that. ▶ I didn't follow what you said. ▶ I'm not sure what you're getting at.	
b Restating (when someone doesn't understand you)	In other words . . . By that, I mean . . .	▶ **A:** There are many ways to engage your audience. **B:** Sorry, but I'm not following. **A:** In other words, you can use your language, voice, and gestures to keep your audience interested. ▶ **A:** Think about the audience. Who are they? Are they co-workers or subordinates? **B:** I'm not sure what you mean by *subordinates*. **A:** By that, I mean people who work for you.
c Checking (when you want to make sure someone understands you)	▶ Just checking—do you know what I mean? ▶ Is that clear? Does anyone have any questions? ▶ Does that make sense?	
d Paraphrasing (what the speaker says)	Are you saying that . . .? If I understood you correctly, you mean that . . . right?	▶ **A:** Successful presenters engage their audience through questions and anecdotes. **B:** Are you saying that the audience is more interested when we include stories in our presentations? ▶ **A:** Cascading goals are important for a business. **B:** If I understood you correctly, you mean that goals are passed down to all levels of an organization, right?
e Paraphrasing (what someone else says)	Narusa said that . . . What . . . means is . . .	▶ Narusa said that setting goals is important for every business. ▶ What Rui means is that we need to be clear about what the company aims to achieve.

Discussion strategies

3 Getting involved

It can be challenging to participate in discussions. Sometimes you have to involve yourself without being asked, keep your turn (if others try to interrupt you), interrupt (when others are talking), and get your turn back (after being interrupted).

Participation strategies	Sample phrases	Examples
a Getting involved	▶ Can I ask a question? ▶ I have something I'd like to contribute to the discussion. ▶ I can offer some input on this topic for us.	
b Keeping your turn	▶ Excuse me, but I'd just like to finish what I'm saying. I'm almost there. ▶ Sorry, but could you give me one more second to finish? ▶ It won't take me long to say this.	
c Interrupting	Excuse me . . . Sorry to interrupt . . . Can I add to . . .	▶ Excuse me, but I'd like to support that idea. ▶ Sorry to interrupt, but I have a question. ▶ Can I add to what you just said?
d Getting your turn back	As I was saying . . . Going back to what I was saying . . . In any case . . .	▶ As I was saying, supervisors should schedule regular talks with their employees. ▶ Going back to what I was saying, it's important to prepare for worst-case scenarios. ▶ In any case, people appreciate being rewarded for their achievements.
e Commenting (on what someone has said)	That's a good point . . . I see what you mean . . . I'm afraid we have different perspectives on this . . .	▶ That's a good point, Elena. ▶ I see what you mean, Jacques. ▶ I'm afraid we have different perspectives on this. I think there is a better way.
f Adding (to what someone has said)	I agree with you . . . and also . . . Another thing to consider is . . . I have something to add to that . . .	▶ I agree with you about customer observations to gain valuable insight, Min, and also, we need to use that insight to design better products. ▶ Yes, and another thing to consider is the best way to test products. ▶ What Min said is true, and I have something to add to that.

Discussion strategies

4 Organizing

Lastly, organization techniques can help communication and make discussion easier to follow.

Organization techniques	Sample words and phrases	Examples
a Chronological	First . . . second . . . third . . .	▶ First, let's talk about the first stage of design thinking . . . empathize. Second, we'll discuss the middle stages . . . define, ideate, and prototype. Third, we'll cover the last stage . . . test.
	Next . . . then . . . later	▶ Next, we'll talk about the five stages of design thinking. Then, we'll look at some examples. Later, we'll discuss how we can use design thinking to design better products.
b Cause and effect	If . . . , then . . .	▶ If you practice healthy thinking, then you can overcome your negative feelings.
	When . . . , then . . .	▶ When you see things positively, then it is easier avoid dwelling on the negative things that happen.
c Categorical	There are [five] stages . . .	▶ There are five stages to the design thinking process.
	The main things . . .	▶ One of the main things to do is to eat a balanced diet.
d Problem and solution	The main problem is . . .	▶ The main problem is that we don't always practice good lifestyle techniques.
	One big issue is . . .	▶ One big issue is that people don't always imagine a successful outcome.
	The best solution is . . .	▶ The best solution is the one that results in a great product.
	We could . . .	▶ We could brainstorm ideas and then discuss which one is best.
e Adding an idea	On top of that . . .	▶ We need to understand each dimension. On top of that, we need to examine suggestions for dealing with cultural differences on the job.
	In the same way, . . .	▶ Personal branding is considered a necessity in today's business world. In the same way, networking is necessary for success.
f Contrast	Although . . .	▶ Although identifying strengths is important, recognizing weaknesses is also useful.
	However . . .	▶ We read and hear information from a lot of different sources every day. However, not all of these sources will be reliable.

VOCABULARY PRACTICE

Vocabulary practice 1

Exercise (A)

Complete the puzzle.

Across

3 free from doubt
6 behavior, way, style
7 feeling superior to others
9 the opposite of speaking clearly
10 only; just; simply

Down

1 leading, impressive
2 to make certain, guarantee
4 in a way that makes you believe it's true
5 agreeable, friendly
8 the opposite of little or limited

Exercise (B)

Use six words from the puzzle to complete the dialogue.

Judy: I know you've given me [1]__________ time to work on this, but I don't think I'm the right person for this project.

Pat: You are! You're [2]__________ unaware of your potential. You should trust yourself more.

Judy: Thank you. You've always been [3]__________ and easy to talk to, and you've never been [4]__________, even when I ask so many questions. And . . . um . . . you know, I, uh . . . really . . .

Pat: Judy, please don't [5]__________! Speak clearly.

Judy: Well, it's just that it looks like I won't be able to finish this by Friday.

Pat: No worries! You can work on it over the weekend and submit it on Monday.

Judy: Really? Oh, thank you! I'll [6]__________ that it's ready by Monday!

Vocabulary practice 2

Exercise (A)

Read the clues and find the words.

Across

1 In order to ________ his speech, he asked a rhetorical question.

6 With his ________ style in his presentation, he managed to keep the audience focused.

7 He thought sharing a humorous story would ________ his presentation.

8 He prepared a final slide in order to ________ the main points from his speech.

10 It wasn't a good idea to ________ so much information on just one slide.

Down

2 As a ________ I avoid a lot of text in my slides.

3 Our manager never treats us like ________; always as equals.

4 The speaker exemplified each of the points with an interesting ________.

5 The ________ speaker immediately captured the audience's attention.

9 Bill raised the ________ of his voice to stress an important point.

Exercise (B)

Use the correct words from the puzzle to complete the notes taken during a talk on effective presentations.

EFFECTIVE PRESENTATIONS TIPS

- audience: co-workers, [1]________, upper management, potential customers, or strangers?
- don't [2]________ slides with charts and graphs and too much information
- change the [3]________ of your voice to stress points
- try to sound [4]________
- engage audience by using a(n) [5]________ or two
- [6]________ your speech using humor
- [7]________ your presentation by summarizing

Vocabulary practice 3

Exercise (A)

Complete the puzzle. What is the vertical word?

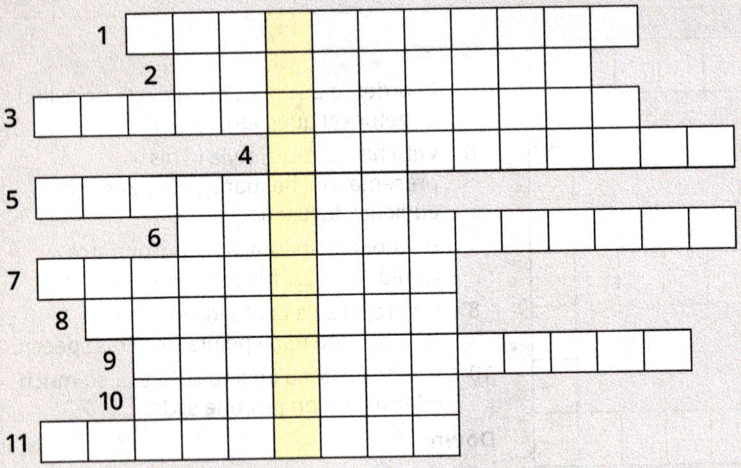

1 It's not easy to ______ all the data, so they use a special program for that.
2 Try to ______ your goals into milestones and monitor your progress towards each goal.
3 Everyone on the team felt motivated after the team leader's ______ speech.
4 The interns are unhappy because it always takes a long time for important news to ______ to them.
5 She didn't want to ______ her team members because she knew that it would affect their productivity.
6 The company's ______ system was too complicated and slowed everything down.
7 ______ of company goals with employees' goals can increase employee engagement and lead to the company's success.
8 The customers found the product old-fashioned and criticized its ______ design.
9 A lack of ______ and trust in a company lead to an unhappy workforce.
10 Strategic goals set at the executive level should ______ down to the rest of the organization.
11 The company needs to consult large shareholders before making any ______ decisions about the company's future.

Exercise (B)

Use the correct words from the puzzle to complete the blog.

Setting and achieving business goals

The first step is to set [1]______ goals that reflect the company's mission and vision. Ensure that the goals are in [2]______ with the overall business plan and are realistic and clear. Each departmental head should then [3]______ these goals down to their managers and employees. It is crucial to monitor and [4]______ the staff's progress with their goals and make other plans if the objectives have not been met, so the goals are still valid and not [5]______. Make sure not to [6]______ anyone with too much to do and [7]______ the work to make it more manageable if necessary. Always provide constructive feedback in [8]______ reviews and encourage [9]______ ideas.

Vocabulary practice 4

Exercise (A)

Complete the puzzle.

Across

2 the opposite of included
5 shared friendship, togetherness
6 promote, encourage
9 absolutely
10 honestly and directly

Down

1 at or from a distance
3 the hidden reason or source of something
4 reimburse
7 a leader in a specific area
8 combination, mixed

Exercise (B)

Use the correct words from the puzzle to complete the dialogue.

Tom: What do you think of the meetings we have on Zoom every month?

Tina: Well, ¹__________, at first, I didn't think ²__________ meetings would be useful, but now I think the opposite. They give everyone the chance to share their ideas, and nobody feels ³__________ or left out because everyone gets a chance to speak. Also, the meetings help ⁴__________ team spirit, especially for those working ⁵__________.

Tom: I agree. And there's a real sense of ⁶__________ when we can speak to one another in real-time. For me, it's almost like we're in the same room!

Vocabulary practice 5

Exercise (A)

Read the clues and find the words and phrases.

B	A	H	F	C	G	P	B	U	N	L	E	A	S	H	P	M
R	I	R	O	A	S	I	Q	F	H	A	O	I	C	W	J	A
A	N	C	E	Z	C	U	L	T	U	R	E	T	O	L	N	R
I	S	I	M	M	E	R	S	I	O	N	U	E	L	D	B	K
N	I	G	P	A	D	Y	E	C	P	O	K	R	L	S	Y	E
S	G	T	A	I	E	A	X	G	D	B	T	A	A	N	C	T
T	H	B	T	N	B	R	E	F	I	N	E	T	B	W	D	S
O	T	N	H	S	Q	E	V	G	Q	H	P	I	O	Q	K	H
R	J	S	I	T	A	S	I	F	X	K	T	O	R	Z	U	A
M	Y	T	Z	R	I	D	E	F	I	N	E	N	A	M	W	R
I	K	A	E	E	L	M	O	P	R	O	T	O	T	Y	P	E
N	E	G	M	A	R	N	V	J	O	D	U	P	I	C	F	Q
G	H	E	R	M	Z	W	A	R	F	L	S	T	V	U	H	V
R	V	S	I	S	Y	N	T	H	E	S	I	Z	E	G	E	J
Z	X	T	H	U	M	B	N	A	I	L	T	J	K	X	L	W
M	U	L	T	I	D	I	S	C	I	P	L	I	N	A	R	Y
S	D	V	M	Z	U	A	Y	N	C	L	B	X	C	Y	I	M

1 involving or combining several fields of study

2 to let loose, free

3 first model, example

4 involvement

5 understanding, knowledge

6 to make something better by making small changes

7 widely accepted

8 collective, shared

9 put oneself in another's place

10 offering ideas and suggestions to find a solution

11 one of many adaptations

12 to put together key ideas from different sources to form a piece of work

Exercise (B)

Use the correct words from the puzzle to complete the speech given by the Design Thinking Team leader.

Understanding our target users is an essential part of the design thinking process. We'll be using various methods to both understand and [1] ____________ with our users. Collectively, these methods will offer us [2] ____________ into our customers' needs. After we gather, analyze, and [3] ____________ the data, we'll have [4] ____________ sessions to come up with ideas. The aim of these sessions is to [5] ____________ our creativity and generate ideas for potential solutions. These potential solutions will lead to creating and testing a(n) [6] ____________. However, even after the testing phase, we'll need to [7] ____________ our product further to offer the best experience to our users.

Vocabulary practice 6

Exercise Ⓐ

Read the clues and find the words.

Across

1 The organizers are hoping to ________ support from local businesses.
4 Nancy's ________ in the face of challenges makes her my role model.
6 The new agreement is ________ to the employees because it protects their rights.
8 It's not easy to boost a group's ________ once it has been damaged.
9 Hillary realized that she needs to ________ regular staff meetings to ensure communication.

Down

2 If the campaign doesn't ________ the public, it won't trigger any response.
3 The text is ________ with the latest statistics.
5 The changes they ________ will completely change how the company works.
7 They will cut expenses and ________ their operations to survive in this weak market.
10 We all should be prepared to change jobs, because ________ could occur at any time.

Exercise Ⓑ

Use the correct words from the puzzle to complete Veronica's email.

Email

Hi Judie,

I finally have good news to share! The company I work for has been going through some difficult times and we were scared that there would be [1] ________ because the managers were saying that they need to [2] ________ and make the company smaller. It seemed like senior management just wasn't able to [3] ________ how to make the company seem more modern and [4] ________. Today, however, our manager held a meeting and really boosted our [5] ________ with a motivational speech. She thanked us for our [6] ________ and shared the news about an upcoming campaign which we hope will [7] ________ more business. I can't wait! I feel it will be really [8] ________ for our company. I'll keep you updated on what happens!

Best,

Veronica

Vocabulary practice 7

Exercise A

Complete the puzzle.

Across

2 crucial, extremely important
5 having important results
6 repeatedly, frequently
8 determination
9 just, only
10 an untested guess

Down

1 disappointed, saddened
3 to disprove
4 accept
7 a person's beliefs and opinions

Exercise B

Use the correct words from the puzzle to complete the text taken from an article about growth mindset.

A growth mindset [1] ____________ means that people believe their talents and intelligence can be improved through effort and actions. This kind of mindset sees "failings" as temporary and changeable and "mistakes" as a [2] ____________ part of learning. Those who adopt a growth mindset respond to mistakes with [3] ____________ and resilience. Even after making the same mistake [4] ____________ people with a growth mindset are less likely to give up than those with fixed mindsets. They believe that even [5] ____________ failures are just temporary setbacks and are a necessary part of the learning process. They also [6] ____________ lifelong learning and believe in constant development. Because they see feedback as an opportunity to learn, they are less likely to be easily [7] ____________.

Vocabulary practice 8

Exercise A

Read the clues and find the words and phrases.

I	A	Y	K	R	M	I	S	I	N	T	E	R	P	R	E	T
N	L	M	I	N	D	F	U	L	I	F	B	E	O	K	O	U
T	V	P	O	V	E	R	S	L	E	E	P	X	S	T	B	E
A	I	H	M	X	Q	J	C	I	C	R	H	P	I	A	S	P
N	S	Q	D	I	S	T	O	R	T	E	D	L	T	D	S	S
G	U	S	L	N	W	F	G	S	A	G	X	A	I	G	E	Y
I	A	Z	A	D	S	O	N	T	D	Q	W	N	V	Z	S	C
B	L	R	D	P	B	P	I	C	E	Z	L	A	E	D	S	H
L	I	Y	V	X	C	N	T	G	Y	I	O	T	L	H	A	O
E	Z	T	I	E	K	F	I	B	V	G	U	I	Y	J	B	L
T	E	M	C	G	Q	W	V	E	M	A	B	O	C	F	O	O
N	U	S	E	V	R	J	E	O	Z	D	E	N	V	B	U	G
R	A	T	I	O	N	A	L	L	Y	A	N	J	H	Y	T	I
O	F	A	L	L	I	N	T	O	T	H	E	T	R	A	P	S
W	U	V	C	O	M	P	A	S	S	I	O	N	K	I	X	T
C	O	N	S	T	R	U	C	T	I	V	E	F	M	L	C	P
J	U	M	P	T	O	C	O	N	C	L	U	S	I	O	N	S

1 to misunderstand, misread

2 opposite of being unaware, unconscious

3 reasonably, logically

4 to think about repeatedly, preoccupy deeply

5 opposite of negatively

6 to behave in a way which is not wise or sensible

7 misrepresented, not completely true

8 an expert or specialist in how the mind works

9 of or relating to the mental processes of perception, memory, judgment, and reasoning

10 sympathy; concern for others

11 to make predictions without sufficient evidence

12 to imagine, picture

Exercise B

Use the correct words or phrases from the puzzle to complete the conversations.

1

When I get upset, I can have a really 1 __________ view of reality and I don't see things clearly.

We all do that. Just be 2 __________ of it when it happens and do something else, like go for a walk.

2

I always 3 __________ what people are going to think when they first meet me. I think about it too much.

You mustn't 4 __________. We can never know what others are going to think.

3

I get scared whenever I'm going to fly and I can't think 5 __________. My mind thinks of the craziest things!

The best thing to do is to 6 __________ your plane landing safely at your destination.

4

I always try to think 7 __________ when I'm around negative people.

Me too. I also try to show them some 8 __________. They're probably very unhappy.

Vocabulary practice 9

Exercise A

Complete the puzzle. What is the vertical word?

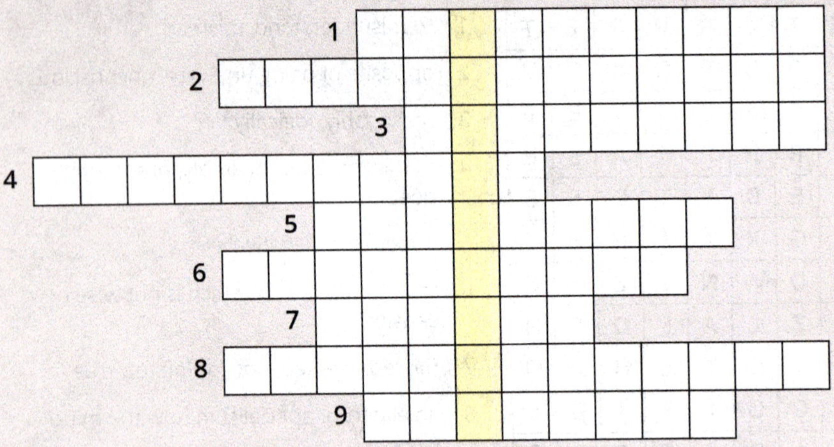

1 controlled, conservative
2 interest in one's own self
3 pleasure-seeking
4 determination, perseverance
5 different from each other
6 in an opposite way
7 careful money management
8 quality of expressing opinions strongly
9 unusual

Exercise B

Use the correct words from the puzzle to complete the dialogue.

1

Anna isn't very 1 __________ when expressing her opinions, is she?

I know, but I like her 2 __________. It shows confidence.

2

My business partner and I have widely 3 __________ opinions on how to develop the company.

I'm sure that with some 4 __________ you can bring him round to your way of thinking.

3

I was very 5 __________ at the weekend, but I had a great time.

Well, that's 6 __________ for you. Perhaps you should do it more often.

4

I really value my manager's 7 __________. He's always honest and genuine.

That's great! 8 __________, I don't believe a word my manager says!

Vocabulary practice 10

Exercise (A)

Read the clues and find the words and phrases.

P	I	N	T	H	E	B	L	A	M	E	O	N	A	M	K
V	A	O	R	A	P	Y	I	Z	D	L	E	B	Y	S	C
T	U	V	K	F	Q	D	M	I	S	M	A	T	C	H	U
R	B	E	Z	B	X	C	I	P	F	I	S	S	U	E	T
U	F	R	T	R	A	I	T	N	C	S	O	H	N	G	T
S	A	S	O	J	I	L	A	J	L	U	J	A	D	Y	I
T	R	E	S	X	B	Q	T	H	C	M	S	W	B	E	N
W	R	L	G	E	X	G	I	A	Z	U	Q	I	M	X	G
O	E	L	I	H	C	W	O	M	V	P	R	K	Z	O	E
R	A	T	T	R	F	I	N	E	T	U	N	E	U	G	D
T	C	W	N	I	M	P	U	L	S	I	V	E	L	Y	G
H	H	C	O	N	T	R	O	V	E	R	S	I	A	L	E
Y	I	N	C	A	P	I	T	A	L	I	Z	E	O	N	F
F	N	O	I	S	F	D	E	X	P	U	Y	V	L	P	W
C	G	T	D	E	V	I	A	T	E	F	R	O	M	T	H
V	M	E	U	R	H	K	D	Q	I	V	E	N	T	G	J

1 to say someone is responsible for something bad

2 characteristic

3 to freely express a negative emotion

4 to not correspond, connect or be the same

5 to use something to your own advantage

6 reliable

7 condition of restricted ability

8 very modern and with all the newest features

9 having a wide range or effect

10 opposite of stay on the course

Exercise (B)

Use the correct words from the puzzle to complete the dialogue.

Joseph: I'm thinking of putting Sylvia in charge of the upcoming project. What do you think?

Mari: If I were you, I wouldn't count on Sylvia. She's not [1]___________ at all.

Joseph: Really? Well, that's not good. Being reliable is the [2]___________ I value most in a team leader.

Mari: Besides, she never admits her mistakes, and she usually tries to [3]___________ others. And if that's not enough, she has been known to [4]___________ her frustration to her colleagues when things go wrong.

Joseph: Then she's definitely not the team leader I'm looking for! I'm surprised to see such a [5]___________ between how she appears and your comments about her, though. How about Tina?

Mari: Well, she's one of the most hardworking members of the team. She also keeps up with the latest trend and knows all about the most [6]___________ technology.

Joseph: Ok, thank you. I'll take your comments into consideration.

Vocabulary practice 11

Exercise A

Complete the puzzle. What is the vertical word?

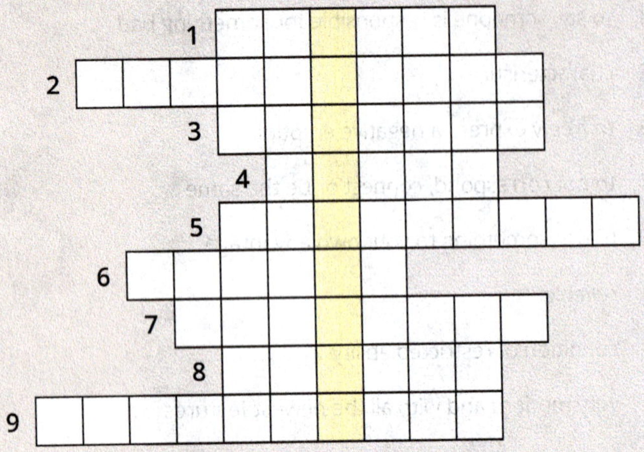

1 They ________ to become a brand that is known around the world.
2 The whole team was disappointed and ________ when things unexpectedly went wrong.
3 Jessica is trying to get her company to ________ her to take a language course because it's quite expensive.
4 They are looking to hire more technically ________ designers for their new gaming division.
5 A good ________ should always do their best to identify and attract suitable candidates to meet companies' needs.
6 The funds available are ________, so we cannot afford to just keep spending.
7 We are usually busy in the morning, but the calls tend to ________ in the afternoon.
8 They have agreed to do it with the ________ that we give them 20% of the money in advance.
9 Mark is well-known for his determination and ________; he recovers easily from any difficulty he faces.

Exercise B

Use the correct words from the puzzle to complete the comment on a blog post.

What is the top quality of an employee? Share your comments!

As a [1] ________, I'm always trying to match people's skills with the company's needs. Of course, most employers need prospective candidates to be computer [2] ________ and up to date with the latest technology, but one of the traits that many companies look for is [3] ________; they want people who can recover quickly from mistakes and setbacks. They don't want employees who get [4] ________ by obstacles and can't move on. They need staff who are [5] ________ about finding solutions to problems and [6] ________ to improve themselves by learning from any difficulties.

Vocabulary practice 12

Exercise (A)

Read the clues and find the words and phrases.

J	Q	V	T	L	Y	P	U	S	H	Y	X	J	Q	M
O	U	P	H	P	U	R	I	O	P	E	S	T	L	D
B	Y	D	R	N	F	O	L	L	O	W	U	P	F	J
H	P	E	E	X	Q	P	T	M	E	T	R	K	E	L
U	R	P	A	N	T	A	G	O	N	I	S	T	I	C
N	O	A	T	O	S	M	U	L	T	I	P	L	E	J
T	S	R	E	B	C	O	U	R	T	E	S	Y	H	I
E	P	T	N	T	S	J	W	F	Z	G	V	D	K	P
R	E	M	I	O	A	F	H	R	S	Y	K	W	Z	V
S	C	E	N	N	C	W	G	T	U	E	C	O	G	I
A	T	N	G	E	E	R	D	I	R	X	B	R	U	E
D	O	T	Z	Q	I	N	T	E	N	S	E	D	I	X
F	C	N	K	H	Y	M	B	V	L	A	W	Y	V	O
N	Z	G	P	R	O	F	E	S	S	I	O	N	A	L
M	D	I	G	E	S	T	A	B	N	C	T	H	W	U

1 Tim is very ________. He disagrees with everything.

2 Employees need time to ________ the major changes the company is making.

3 Ryan is not competitive; I don't think he will ________ for the manager's position.

4 Armand never lets me finish a sentence without interrupting. He is a real ________!

5 Obviously, she was trying to motivate us, but she was too ________. She needs to relax a little.

6 I don't think there is any ________ of promotion in this office, so I'm leaving

7 Most ________ have been struggling to find well-paid jobs.

8 Dad gave a(n) ________ look to the kids, so they ran off immediately.

9 Diana's ________ text was too long and impossible to understand.

10 He can be very ________ sometimes. He often frightens his colleagues.

11 He doesn't even have the common ________ to say, "Good morning," when he comes into the office.

Exercise (B)

Use the correct words from the puzzle to complete the dialogue.

Tracy: Have you heard anything about your interview?

Matt: No, nothing. I sent a follow-up email, but they haven't had the [1]____________ to reply. Maybe I should send another one.

Tracy: Well, recruiters don't often send replies. They're very busy. I wouldn't send another one, if I were you. You don't want to become a [2]____________.

Matt: Yeah, I guess. It's just so frustrating. I'm having to [3]____________ with so many candidates for each job I apply to. But I really want this job! I'm perfect for it! If only I could make them see that.

Tracy: You need to relax. Were you this [4]____________ in your follow-up email?

Matt: I don't know . . . maybe. In my last email, I wrote a page and a half about how I was perfect for the job.

Tracy: Oh no! [5]____________ emails won't help you get you hired. You should always keep follow-up emails short. Otherwise, you will come across as too [6]____________.

Glossary

Module 1: Communication 1

filler (n) usually meaningless words and sounds that we use without realizing when we are speaking
upcoming (adj) happening soon

Module 2: Communication 2

thought-provoking (adj) making people think seriously about a particular subject

Module 3: Goal Setting

employee retention (phr) keeping employees motivated so that they keep working for the same company

Module 4: Teamwork

on-site (adj) at the place or on the area of land that you are talking about

Module 5: Critical Thinking

market share (phr) the percentage of shares in a market that a company or product has
thumbnail sketch (phr) a short description that gives only the main facts about a person, thing, or event
work culture (phr) employee behavior and attitude within a company

Module 6: Leadership

Diversity and Inclusion (phr) two interconnected concepts that refer to the variety of unique individuals and the environment that allows them to work together as equally valid contributors.
economic downturn (phr) a period or process in which business activity, production etc. is reduced and economic conditions become worse
shoestring budget (phr) very little budget to spend

Module 7: Self-Management

hysterically (adv) doing something in a way that you are unable to control your behavior or emotions because you are very upset, afraid, excited etc.
intolerant (adj) not willing to accept ways of thinking and behaving that are different from your own

Module 8: Wellness

intangible (adj) an intangible quality or feeling is difficult to describe exactly
oversleep (v) to sleep for longer than you intended

Module 9: Social Responsibility

high-end (adj) relating to products or services that are more expensive and of better quality than other products of the same type
indulgence (n) something that you do or have for pleasure, not because you need it

Module 10: Branding

impulsively (adv) doing something without considering the possible dangers or problems first
oversell (v) to praise someone or something too much

Module 11: Job Search

corporate ladder (phr) a series of levels which someone moves up and down within an organization, profession, or society
freelance (adj) working independently for different companies rather than being employed by one particular company
invoice (n) a list of goods that have been supplied or work that has been done, showing how much you owe for them
job hopping (phr) when someone changes their job very often
leverage (v) to spread or use resources or ideas in several different ways or in different parts of a company, system etc.

Module 12: Interviewing

off-putting (adj) if someone's behavior or the appearance of something is off-putting, you do not like it or you think it is unattractive
prompt (adj) at the right time without being late

Notes